THE
Ketogenic
Diet Cookbook

AMANDA C. HUGHES

WickedStuffed.com

THE Ketogenic Diet Cookbook

Easy, Whole Food Keto Recipes
for Any Budget

FALL RIVER PRESS

New York

FALL RIVER PRESS

New York

An Imprint of Sterling Publishing Co., Inc.
1166 Avenue of the Americas
New York, NY 10036

For information about custom editions, special sales, and premium and corporate purchases, please
contact Sterling Special Sales at 800-805-5489 or specialsales@sterlingpublishing.com.

Manufactured in China

4 6 8 10 9 7 5 3

sterlingpublishing.com

Image credits:
Stocksy/Nadine Greeff, Cover; Stockfood/Mick Jones, p.2; Stockfood/Helen Catchcart, p.6;
Stocksy/Darren Muir, p.9; Stockfood/Victoria Firmston, p.10; Stocksy/Laura Adani, p.28; Stocksy/
Ina Peters, p.28; Stockfood/Mona Binner, p.82; Stockfood/Jalag/Schuerle Grossman, p.100; Stocksy/
Jeff Wasserman, p.124; Stockfood/Andre Baranowski, p.170; Stockfood/Gräfe & Unzer Verlag/Joerg
Lehrmann, p.194; Stockfood/The Stepford Husband, p.214; Stockfood/Noel Barnhurst, p.236; Stockfood/
Gräfe & Unzer Verlag/Joerg Lehrmann, Backcover; Stockfood/Andrew Baranowski, Backcover

To Patrick, my partner in love, life, and ketosis.
And to my goldendoodle Napa, who doesn't mind
cleaning up our leftovers.

Contents

Introduction

For most people, ice cream is the cure-all that can mend a bad day, a broken heart, and a sunburn. While chocolate-chip cookie-dough ice cream has been there for me through thick and thin, it's the ketogenic diet that has saved me from bigger issues, like being overweight, having chronic vertigo, and feeling the type of anxiety where it always feels like the room is spinning.

In 2010, my now husband learned about the ketogenic diet through social media. When he described the diet, where fat and protein are the primary components, I told him he was crazy. How could anyone survive without spaghetti or macaroni and cheese? What about *cake*? When he said he was going to try it, I begged him not to and told him that I'd never forgive him if he dropped dead from a heart attack from this crazy bacon and butter diet.

Thankfully for both of us, he was patient with my clear over-reaction and, instead, started sending me articles on the benefits of a ketogenic diet for a variety of health issues. When I read the parts about reduced anxiety, I was intrigued. But when I learned how the reduction of sugar in your body could starve cancer, I willingly did my own research. Fast-forward to today, and I've lost almost a hundred pounds (most of it in the first few years, with more still to go), and my vertigo is virtually nonexistent. I sleep great at night, wake up early, have energy throughout the day, am mentally clear instead of in a constant brain fog, and feel like a new person. My cholesterol levels are as good as they've ever been, and my triglycerides are cut in half.

The ketogenic diet was and still is the only "diet" I've been on. I like to think of it as more of a lifestyle change because it truly does touch all parts of my life—and changed the way I live.

I've spent the last several years developing a whole food–focused approach to the ketogenic diet for myself. If you're putting all this work into losing weight and getting healthy, why not use the healthiest ingredients you can?

It's for this reason you'll find that my recipes are less likely to use typical "low-carb" products, even sweeteners like erythritol and stevia, unless necessary, and why I often recommend organic vegetables and grass-fed beef. By all means substitute conventional ingredients to stay within your budget, but, when you have the option, go for organic veggies that don't use pesticides, and grass-fed beef, which has abundant healthy, anti-inflammatory omega-3s. "Organic" isn't a marketing word; it distinguishes high-quality ingredients. ("All-natural" and "artisan," on the other hand, aren't regulated designations and are purely marketing terms.)

For many years I've shared my whole food recipes with other ketoers on my blog, WickedStuffed.com, and together we've come up with new and creative ways to approach meals that don't include bread, sugar, and other additives. In this book, you'll find the results of years of experimenting with new flavors and ingredients. My recipes are usually simple and include pantry staples, but I'll also introduce you to some of my favorite keto ingredients like ghee, burrata, and pink Himalayan salt. I hope you have as much fun preparing—and eating—the recipes in this book as I did creating them.

CHAPTER ONE

THE WHOLE FOOD KETOGENIC LIFESTYLE

The ketogenic diet can be as simple or as complicated as you make it. In its simplest form, it can be described as staying in ketosis. Ketosis is the process by which your body creates ketones for energy in the absence of carbohydrates. Cave people didn't indulge in boxes of mini brownies; they got their energy from vegetables, berries, and meat. To get in and stay in ketosis, most ketoers start by eating fewer than 20 net carbohydrates per day. Ketogenic dieters also try to keep their daily macronutrient intake (or "macros") at about 10 percent carbs, 20 percent protein, and 70 percent fats. You'll see this is easier than you think. Once you determine how many carbs you can consume before kicking yourself out of ketosis, you may find you can raise the bar from 20 to 50 net carbohydrates per day.

Back when men and women foraged for food, they hunted birds and animals, caught fish, and snagged fruits and berries off plants. With the discovery and refinement of sugar, energy could suddenly be produced from carbohydrates, which are easy to process and turn into energy. However, they also burn off—and are thus wasted—just as quickly.

Before humans began ingesting refined sugar and carbohydrates, we were always in ketosis. Paleo advocates suggest that back then, our bodies were fueled by ketones for energy and burned fat for fuel. Even today, significant amounts of carbohydrates aren't needed. In fact, according to a 2002 study published in the *Journal of Pediatrics*, babies are born in ketosis and stay that way for as long as they're breastfeeding. This also happens to be the time when babies' brains are growing at a tremendous rate. You may not feel hungry while in ketosis because your food is digested and energy is burned more slowly. Basically, you're getting more bang for your food buck.

The ketogenic diet was not developed for weight loss, but as a very real remedy for patients with epilepsy, and it is recommended by the Epilepsy Foundation. But, according to a 2004 study published in the *Journal of the International Society of Sports Nutrition*, a ketogenic diet does support weight loss. Indeed, many weight-loss diets, including Atkins, were built upon its principles. The South Beach diet is a low-carb diet, but its goal is to keep you slightly out of ketosis. Paleo can be considered ketogenic, but anyone consuming honey and quinoa is not likely in ketosis either. In some ways you could call the ketogenic diet the blueprint for all low-carb diets. People have used it success-fully for weight loss, but also for reducing anxiety and increasing energy and mental clarity. In addition, a 2013 study published in the *European Journal of Clinical Nutrition* showed that it may even help pre-vent acne, Parkinson's disease, multiple sclerosis, and cancer.

No matter your journey, the recipes in this book are ketogenic-compliant—meaning they are naturally low in carbs—and may help with one, or all, of the preceding ailments. And your belly will feel full all the while!

Keto Nutrition

The ketogenic diet is simple in its implementation (goal: stay in ketosis); however, the path can be different for each person. Everyone begins at 20 net carbohydrates and then, over time, determines how many they can consume without being kicked out of ketosis. I've eaten as much as 75 net carbs in a day and stayed in ketosis (it was Disney World, there was funnel cake, enough said) while my husband, who stuck to his diet and had two bites, was kicked out of ketosis. Everyone is different, of course. It's up to each of us to learn what our personal "kick out" point is and stay below it.

How do you know if you are in ketosis? Simple: keto sticks. Tubes of these thin test strips are available at your local pharmacy. Simply urinate on a stick to find out if you're in or out of ketosis. If the stick turns light pink, you're out of ketosis; any shade of purple means you're in. Note that a darker shade of purple does not indicate "better" ketosis—it matters only if you are in or out, burning fat or not. There aren't tiers or levels you need to reach. However, if you're diabetic, you run the risk of a condition called ketoacidosis on a ketogenic diet. Be sure to talk with your doctor about the diet; he or she will likely recommend using keto sticks and making sure you stay in the light purple range.

To calculate net carbohydrates, take the number of carbohydrates you consume and subtract the number of fiber grams consumed. This is the number you'll use to track your daily total. When food is high in fiber, like coconut, you can eat more of it even if the carbohydrate numbers look a little scary.

When I refer to macros, I'm talking about the balance of foods you eat in a day as they fall into one of the three main macronutrient categories: carbohydrates, proteins, and fat. Some people on the keto diet find that these percentages are helpful for keeping track of their weight loss, and other people use them for medical reasons. If you don't have any medical reasons to stick to certain percentages, then I think a good daily starting point for the ketogenic diet is 10 percent carbs, 20 percent proteins, and 70 percent fats. If this doesn't keep you in ketosis, try 5 percent carbs, 15 percent proteins, and 80 percent fats. Ultimately, it's up to you to find the balance that works best for you.

There are hundreds of calculators online that you can use to input your stats, such as weight, height, sex, weight goal, and so on, and the calculator will tell you what is supposed to be the ideal macro for you. The amount of carbs (which should generally come from vegetables) or fats that will create ketosis in the body varies for different people. It is certainly not an exact science.

For the recipes in this book, the macro percentages were calculated by taking the number of grams of each macro and multiplying it by the number of calories per gram (9 calories for 1 gram of fat, 4 calories for 1 gram of carbs or proteins) and then dividing that by the total number of calories per serving. For example, imagine a dish that has the following nutritional information per serving:

Calories: 184; Total Fat: 14g; Saturated Fat: 6g; Cholesterol: 224mg; Carbohydrates: 2g; Fiber: 1g; Net Carbs: 1g; Protein: 12g

To determine how much of a serving's calories come from fat:

(14 grams of fat) × (9 calories per gram of fat) = 126 calories from fat

(126 calories from fat per serving) ÷ (184 total calories per serving) = 68.5%

To determine how much of a serving's calories come from total carbs (not net carbs):

(2 grams of carbs) × (4 calories per gram of carb) = 8 calories from carbs

(8 calories from carbs per serving) ÷ (184 total calories per serving) = 4%

To determine how much of a serving's calories come from protein:

(12 grams of protein) × (4 calories per gram of protein) = 48 calories from protein

(48 calories from protein per serving) ÷ (184 total calories per serving) = 26%

KETO VERSUS PALEO

To follow a strict ketogenic diet, you will need to consume no more than 20 net carbohydrates a day (most Americans eat closer to 300). While no foods are off-limits, many ketoers choose not to eat sugar, bread, and grains. Their carbs come instead from whole foods like vegetables. Proteins are also consumed, but healthy fats make up much of the meal plans.

The paleo diet is meant to mimic the diet of early humans, which did not include refined sugars, grains, and dairy. The idea is that the foods of our early ancestors—protein, vegetables, and fruits—provided all the necessary nutrients and energy. The sugars, grains, and dairy we consume today are linked to food allergies and intolerances, as well as the increase in celiac disease, diabetes, and lactose intolerance, among other ailments.

While the paleo diet can often be ketogenic, the ketogenic diet is not necessarily paleo. The keto diet doesn't preclude certain foods—you simply won't want to waste your carbs on them. The goal of the keto diet is only to stay in ketosis, so any of these foods at low levels likely won't kick you out. These same principles apply to the recipes in this book. You won't find any grains or sugars here, but you'll find plenty of dairy—delicious, wonderful dairy. However, if you're going the paleo route, keep an eye out for my "Make it paleo" tips, which are provided wherever possible.

Every meal you eat doesn't need to follow these macros; you make a tally at the end of the day. This allows you to eat a dish of vegetables sautéed in ghee without the need to throw in pancetta (unless you want to).

As you consult the macros for each recipe in this book, be aware that there's variation among different ingredients. For example, organic heavy cream may have less than 1 net carb, while a non-organic store brand may have more. Tomato sauce is another tricky one. Some better varieties of marinara come in as low as 4 net carbs per ¼ cup because they contain no added sugar, but most mainstream brands have 15 or more net carbs in that same ¼ cup. To enjoy an Italian fix now and again, I recommend splurging on the good stuff— or making your own sauce.

Although the ketogenic diet is not meant to be exclusionary, and you could certainly get your 20 net carbs each day from a single slice of bread, you probably won't make it far in a ketogenic lifestyle. Your blood sugar will spike and probably kick you out of ketosis, and it won't be any fun. Try instead some buttery veggies and ooey-gooey fondue, and that slice of bread won't be necessary. Just wait and see: Before long you will lose your cravings for bread!

Diet Guidelines

Following are some of the best ways to stay in ketosis and get the most out of your ketogenic experience. These tips will help you survive what's known as "keto flu." During your first few days, or up to a week, of ketosis, you may feel a bit tired, sluggish, and dizzy as your body adjusts to producing and burning ketones as energy instead of carbohydrates. (In the Atkins diet, this period is known as "induction.")

Stick to your macros. The daily 10/20/70 ratio is worth sticking to because it works. Too many carbs and you won't burn fat. Too much protein and it won't burn off if you don't use it. Not enough fat and you won't be full. All these problems add up to less energy. The recommended ratio allows for a whole food approach to ketosis that includes alkalizing green veggies, which break down the acids in meat.

Keep your electrolytes up. Electrolytes are the minerals in our blood that keep us hydrated and keep our nerves and muscles working properly in balance. By producing ketones, you'll be flushing out more electrolytes than usual. This means you should increase your salt intake while following keto because your body won't hang onto sodium like it used to. Most ketoers do this by drinking chicken broth or bouillon daily, especially in the first few weeks of ketosis while the body is adjusting. If you feel achy in the first week on keto while going through carbohydrate withdrawal, bouillon helps. Many ketoers use magnesium supplements as well.

Drink lots of water. Drinking water is one of those things that everyone tells you to do, and you don't take it seriously until you end up with a kidney stone! I promise that drinking two to three liters of water every day will make your body feel clean, full, and hydrated; keep your bowels moving; and help you lose weight faster if that's what you're ketoing for.

Keep track of what you eat. Measuring what you eat turns any diet into a game. Use apps like MyFitnessPal to track your meals and measure your macros at the end of the day. There's also an app called Quip you can use to make shopping lists. It includes check marks that allow you to reuse your shopping list every week.

REMEMBER TO CHECK INGREDIENT LISTS!

The following products are often sold with added sugars or fillers, so check labels carefully before purchasing, and remember to calculate the net carbs by subtracting the amount of fiber from the total amount of carbohydrates. You need items that are low in net carbs. The following foods are used often in my recipes, and I've listed my favorite brands, too.

1. Peanut butter. Many brands have too much sugar, so choose a brand that is low in net carbs. My favorite is the Teddie brand of peanut butter, which has only 4 net carbs per serving. Most organic peanut butters that contain only peanuts will match or even beat this number.

2. Organic dairy products. Organic heavy (whipping) cream, sour cream, and cream cheese don't have any carbs, or less than 1 carb. Their nonorganic counterparts can have 2 or even 3 net carbs per serving. I like Organic Valley brand.

3. Tomato sauce. If you pick any tomato sauce off the supermarket shelf, you'll find it has anywhere from 10 to 20 net carbs per serving. Stick with one that doesn't have added sugar and contains less than 4 net carbs per serving. Two popular brands are Mezzetta and Rao's.

4. Coconut milk is good and fatty, but unsweetened coconut milk has 1 net carb or less, as compared to 9 or more per serving for regular coconut milk.

5. Whey protein powder can be very high in sugar, but there are many low- and no-carb brands on the market.

6. Prepared foods offered at your favorite grocery store often include sugar and breading that you can't see by looking at them.

7. Frozen hamburgers often use fillers and might carry 3 to 5 carbs per burger, when it would be 0 if you make them yourself from pure ground beef.

8. "Sugar-free" does not always translate to low-carb, and "gluten-free" almost never means low-carb. In fact, low-carb isn't always ketogenic. You may find 20 to 30 carbs in a low-carb bagel!

9. Salad dressings can be loaded with sugar, so look for those with 0 to 1 net carb per serving.

10. Pre-cut cheese, especially American cheese, is often loaded with up to 3 carbs per slice! Stick with organic shredded cheese containing no fillers, and you'll be left with less than 1 net carb per serving.

11. Deli meat is rarely low-carb. A small serving of bologna could be 5 carbs or more. When you do indulge in deli meats with fewer carbs (such as turkey, chicken, and ham), buy nitrate-free varieties.

Eat your calories. Don't try to do a low-calorie ketogenic diet, or you'll end up without any fuel. Fat is your new fuel. Without it, you'll not only be hungry, but you also won't lose weight. Many ketoers eat 1,800 calories or more per day, and I find that eating less actually makes me *stop* losing weight. But don't overindulge, either. You won't likely lose weight eating 5,000 calories a day. The good news is that you won't be hungry enough to eat that much anyway!

Stock up on healthy fats. Fat has become a dirty word in our society. But there are plenty of good fats out there. Cook everything in ghee, which is lactose- and casein-free clarified butter, high in anti-inflammatory omega-3 fatty acids. For times when you run out of this magical golden buttery oil, keep a backup of coconut oil and olive oil. Avoid processed oils like vegetable, sunflower seed, soybean, and corn—they are high in inflammatory omega-6s, which in turn destroy the healthy omega-3s in your body.

Invest in certified organic, grass-fed, and free-range products. I'm not trying to go all crunchy granola on you, but now that your diet is exchanging highly refined carbohydrates for mostly fats and proteins, you'll want to pay extra-special attention to the quality of those ingredients. I'll identify such ingredients in most of the recipes, and I recommend you buy them if your budget allows.

Stick to real food, not low-carb products. If you check the label of most low-carb products, unless they're also paleo products, you'll be shocked at their ingredients, such as unpronounceable chemical additives. You can control what goes into your body by making your own meals and sticking to whole foods.

Foods to Enjoy

High Fat / Low Carb (based on net carbs)

Meats & Seafood

BEEF
(ground beef, steak, etc.)

CHICKEN

CRAB

CRAWFISH

DUCK

FISH

GOOSE

LAMB

LOBSTER

MUSSELS

OCTOPUS

PORK
(pork chops, bacon, etc.)

QUAIL

SAUSAGE
(without fillers)

SCALLOPS

SHRIMP

VEAL

VENISON

Dairy

BLUE CHEESE DRESSING

BURRATA CHEESE

COTTAGE CHEESE

CREAM CHEESE

EGGS

GREEK YOGURT
(full-fat)

GRILLING CHEESE

HALLOUMI CHEESE

HEAVY (WHIPPING) CREAM

HOMEMADE WHIPPED CREAM

KEFALOTYRI CHEESE

MOZZARELLA CHEESE

PROVOLONE CHEESE

QUESO BLANCO

RANCH DRESSING

RICOTTA CHEESE

UNSWEETENED ALMOND MILK

UNSWEETENED COCONUT MILK

Nuts & Seeds

ALMONDS

BRAZIL NUTS

CHIA SEEDS

FLAXSEED

HAZELNUTS

MACADAMIA NUTS

PEANUTS
(in moderation)

PECANS

PINE NUTS

PUMPKIN SEEDS

SACHA INCHI SEEDS

SESAME SEEDS

WALNUTS

Fruits & Vegetables

ALFALFA SPROUTS

ASPARAGUS

AVOCADOS

BELL PEPPERS

BLACKBERRIES

BLUEBERRIES

BROCCOLI

CABBAGE

CARROTS
(in moderation)

CAULIFLOWER

CELERY

CHICORY

COCONUT

CRANBERRIES

CUCUMBERS

GARLIC
(in moderation)

GREEN BEANS

HERBS

JICAMA

LEMONS

LIMES

MUSHROOMS

OKRA

OLIVES

ONIONS
(in moderation)

PICKLES

PUMPKIN

RADISHES

RASPBERRIES

SALAD GREENS

SCALLIONS

SPAGHETTI SQUASH
(in moderation)

STRAWBERRIES

TOMATOES
(in moderation)

ZUCCHINI

Foods to Avoid

Low Fat / High Carb (based on net carbs)

Meats & Meat Alternatives

DELI MEAT
(some, not all)

HOT DOGS
(with fillers)

SAUSAGE
(with fillers)

SEITAN

TOFU

Dairy

ALMOND MILK
(sweetened)

COCONUT MILK
(sweetened)

MILK

SOY MILK
(regular)

YOGURT
(regular)

Nuts & Seeds

CASHEWS

CHESTNUTS

PISTACHIOS

Fruits & Vegetables

APPLES

APRICOTS

ARTICHOKES

BANANAS

BEANS
(all varieties)

BOYSENBERRIES

BURDOCK ROOT

BUTTERNUT SQUASH

CANTALOUPE

CHERRIES

CHICKPEAS

CORN

CURRANTS

DATES

EDAMAME

EGGPLANT

ELDERBERRIES

GOOSEBERRIES

GRAPES

HONEYDEW MELON

HUCKLEBERRIES

KIWIS

LEEKS

MANGOS

ORANGES

PARSNIPS

PEACHES

PEAS

PINEAPPLES

PLANTAINS

PLUMS

POTATOES

PRUNES

RAISINS

SWEET POTATOES

TARO ROOT

TURNIPS

WATER CHESTNUTS

WINTER SQUASH

YAMS

Ten Tips for Keeping Keto Costs Down

Paying higher prices for grass-fed, free-range, organic foods buys you peace of mind on the ketogenic diet. These types of products are generally higher in good fatty acids and lower in not-so-great ones. If you're splurging on high-quality products, here's how you can cut costs elsewhere.

1. **Buy from a butcher or local farmer.** Butcher shops tend to be less expensive than most supermarkets, and you can also get excellent, less-costly cuts like the lesser-known tri-tip. If you're cooking for the whole family or simply want lots of leftovers, make the slow cooker your friend and take advantage of roasts instead of single cuts of meat. If you have ample freezer space, consider buying a whole cow— seriously. Many farmers sell whole, half, or quarter cows and will butcher the meat and vacuum-seal every cut for you.

2. **Shop every week.** When you come home to an empty fridge, it's hard to resist the urge to dine out or order in. But to do so while following a ketogenic diet usually means you're getting a cheap salad or an expensive steak, and nobody ever goes for the salad when they're hungry after a long day. A well-stocked fridge translates to nutritious meals for far less money than eating out.

3. **Create a meal plan.** On the ketogenic diet, you won't need most dried and packaged goods. Instead, you'll be buying a lot of fresh produce, meats, and dairy products that don't have a very long shelf life. Plan a week's worth of meals, along with a shopping list, and avoid veering from that list. By following a plan and a list, you'll avoid wasting food by buying only what you need.

4. **Shop the sales and cheaper cuts of meat.** You don't need to eat grass-fed ribeye steaks every day. If beef isn't on sale, look for less expensive options like chicken legs or pork chops. You can easily feed a family of four for under $5 if you buy meat on sale.

5. **Splurge on the essentials now.** Buy staples like ghee, coconut oil, pink Himalayan salt (if you can find it), Maldon sea salt, and dried herbs and spices in bulk from discount outlets. Your pantry will be well stocked, and your week-to-week grocery bill won't get blown up with tiny $15 jars of coconut oil at the grocery store. Most of these products have long shelf lives, and a little goes a long way, so it will be a while before you need to restock.

6. **Make your own.** Lots of recipes call for chicken broth. Next time you roast a chicken, make your own bone broth (see the recipe on page 193). Strain the broth through cheesecloth and freeze individual portions for future recipes. Instead of buying fresh herbs every week, make herbal ice cubes. Mince fresh herb(s) and pack them into ice cube trays so that each cube is about ¾ full. Fill the trays with boiling water to blanch the herbs and put them in the freezer. Pop the ice cubes out when they're frozen and store them in freezer bags.

7. **Invest in a vacuum sealer.** When you buy meat in bulk, make it last longer with a vacuum sealer. I even marinate my meats with spices and herbs (but not salt) before freezing.

8. **Focus on cheaper ingredients.** A whole food approach to the ketogenic diet doesn't mean meat every night. Tuna salad on romaine lettuce leaves, or slices of tomato and mozzarella drizzled with herbs, olive oil, and balsamic vinegar is far more budget friendly and equally delicious.

9. **Buy in season.** Imported strawberries are expensive in December, but in the summer you can get them at even the most expensive farm stand for under $3 a container. Buy in season and save on the fruits and vegetables that are abundant at different times of the year.

10. **Make recipes with fewer ingredients.** I've tried to eliminate unnecessary ingredients, like an herb garnish, unless it serves a culinary purpose other than looking pretty. (Fresh herbs are indeed lovely, but often only a small amount is needed. Freeze the remaining herbs

in some water in an ice cube tray, or in a tightly packed and sealed plastic bag.) You can cherry-pick the recipes you make based on the ingredients required. Ingredients that tend to increase the cost of a recipe include fresh herbs, fancy cheeses, and wine.

The Recipes

The ketogenic recipes in this book are as close as we can get to a whole food approach to keto while still keeping it delicious every step of the way. Always pay close attention to the nutrition labels on any packaged foods to make sure you're choosing those with no added sugars or fillers. When I've included such ingredients in recipes, it's because you can easily find naturally low-carb versions in most stores.

You can identify more affordable recipes in this book from the price scale included with each, ranging from 💰 ($5 or less for the whole recipe) to 💰💰💰💰 (expensive ingredients for a special meal). This scale is a comparison of the recipes in this book only.

I've also included the macro data for each recipe, plus nutritional information for calories, fat, fiber, carbohydrates, net carbohydrates, and protein.

Paleo-friendly recipes are marked as 🍖. When other recipes can be made paleo friendly, you'll find a "Make it paleo" tip that guides you to the appropriate substitutions.

GHEE

A prerequisite to cooking the delicious recipes in this book is that you go out and get yourself a large jar of ghee. Not olive oil, not even coconut oil, but ghee. Ghee is butter that has been cooked to remove milk proteins, sugars, and water. You'll find grass-fed ghee called for in a large number of my recipes thanks to its ability to be used as both an oil and as a butter. It's paleo friendly and has a better ratio of omega-6 to omega-3 fatty acids (1.6 to 1) than olive oil (12.8 to 1). I eat it by the spoonful, and it's encouraged for digestion in many cultures. It's also delicious.

You can find ghee at your local natural foods grocery or Indian foods store. I often order mine online from Tin Star Foods (www.tinstarfoods.com), which produces the best-tasting ghee I've ever had, but you can also make it yourself using my Golden Ghee recipe on page 224.

CHAPTER TWO
BREAKFAST

TOASTED CINNAMON-
VANILLA-COCONUT CEREAL

SERVES 4 / PREP TIME: 5 MINUTES / COOK TIME: 5 MINUTES

2 cups unsweetened shaved coconut

½ cup crushed walnuts

1 vanilla bean, seeds scraped out

Ground cinnamon

Powdered stevia

Unsweetened almond milk

KETO TIP *Coconut is high in carbs in large quantities, but it's full of the good fats you need, so you can get full on just a little.*

Cinnamon is a natural sweetener, so when you're missing cereal, look no further than this crunchy alternative to sugary breakfast bowls. All you need is ½ cup with unsweetened almond milk. The fiber-rich coconut will fill you up all morning.

1. Preheat the oven to 350°F.

2. Line a rimmed baking sheet with parchment paper.

3. Spread out the coconut and walnuts in an even layer on the prepared sheet. Toast in the oven until light brown, about 5 minutes.

4. As soon as the coconut and walnuts come out of the oven, sprinkle them with the vanilla bean seeds, cinnamon, and stevia and toss to evenly coat. Taste and adjust the flavor as desired with more cinnamon, stevia, or both.

5. Put ½ cup of this cereal in a bowl and pour in your preferred amount of unsweetened almond milk. Serve immediately. Store any unused cereal in an airtight container at room temperature.

———

PER SERVING (WITHOUT THE ALMOND MILK): CALORIES: 239; TOTAL FAT: 14G; SATURATED FAT: 0G; PROTEIN: 4G; CHOLESTEROL: 0MG; CARBOHYDRATES: 8G; FIBER: 5G; **NET CARBS: 3G**

FAT: 73% / CARBS: 18% / PROTEIN: 9%

CINNAMON TOAST PORK RINDS

SERVES 1 / PREP TIME: 5 MINUTES

I was surprised to discover that pork rinds can take on the flavor of whatever they're coated in—even a cinnamon and sugarlike mix. Crush these up and add some unsweetened almond milk for a bowl of ketogenic breakfast cereal!

In a small bowl, stir together the heavy cream, vanilla stevia, cinnamon, nutmeg, and salt (if using). Stir in the pork rinds and enjoy.

PER SERVING: CALORIES: 483; TOTAL FAT: 37G;
SATURATED FAT: 20G; PROTEIN: 35G; CHOLESTEROL: 97MG;
CARBOHYDRATES: 1G; FIBER: 1G; **NET CARBS: 0G**

FAT: 70% / CARBS: 1% / PROTEIN: 29%

¼ cup organic heavy (whipping) cream

2 drops liquid vanilla stevia

½ teaspoon ground cinnamon

⅛ teaspoon ground nutmeg

¼ teaspoon sea salt (optional)

1 cup crushed pork rinds

MAKE IT PALEO *Heavy cream sticks particularly well to the pork rinds, but you can use unsweetened almond milk instead.*

OATLESS RICOTTA OATMEAL

SERVES 1 / PREP TIME: 5 MINUTES / COOK TIME: 1 MINUTE

½ cup organic
ricotta cheese

4 tablespoons salted
grass-fed butter

⅛ teaspoon ground
cinnamon

Sweetener to taste

I didn't miss oatmeal until it was gone. I hadn't eaten oatmeal for years before keto, but once it was out of the picture, I was running back to it like an ex-boyfriend I forgot I barely liked. I thought, "A nice hot bowl of oatmeal would be delicious. Wait, who am I? What year is this?" But some keto friends told me about this hack and, when I tried it, I was hooked. It really does achieve a similar texture to oatmeal or cream of wheat.

In a small microwave-safe bowl, mix the ricotta cheese, butter, cinnamon, and sweetener. Heat it in the microwave until hot, about 1 minute.

PER SERVING: CALORIES: 578; TOTAL FAT: 56G;
SATURATED FAT: 35G; PROTEIN: 15G; CHOLESTEROL: 161MG;
CARBOHYDRATES: 1G; FIBER: 0G; **NET CARBS: 1G**

FAT: 89% / CARBS: 1% / PROTEIN: 10%

LEMON-LAVENDER RICOTTA PANCAKES

SERVES 2 / PREP TIME: 5 MINUTES / COOK TIME: 10 MINUTES

This recipe is my ode to Caffe Dolce Vita in Providence, Rhode Island, and their lemon-lavender pancakes with lemon-lavender butter and my lemon-lavender love. It's like eating the entire region of Napa Valley.

1. In a blender, combine the eggs, ricotta cheese, sweetener, lemon juice, coconut flour, lavender, and baking powder. Blend on low for 10 seconds.

2. In a medium skillet, melt the ghee over medium heat. Pour about ¼ cup of the batter into the center of the pan. Cook the pancake until the bottom is brown and crispy, about 1 minute. Flip the pancake and cook the other side until brown and crispy, 30 seconds to 1 minute more. Repeat this step to cook 3 more pancakes.

3. Sprinkle each serving with the lemon zest and top the pancakes with a pat of butter. Serve with your favorite keto-friendly sugar-free maple syrup.

PER SERVING: CALORIES: 279; TOTAL FAT: 20G;
SATURATED FAT: 10G; PROTEIN: 18G; CHOLESTEROL: 398MG;
CARBOHYDRATES: 5G; FIBER: 3G; **NET CARBS: 2G**

FAT: 65% / CARBS: 7% / PROTEIN: 28%

4 large free-range eggs

¼ cup organic ricotta cheese

2 teaspoons Sugar-Free Vanilla Bean Sweetener (page 196)

1 teaspoon freshly squeezed Meyer lemon juice

2 tablespoons coconut flour

1 tablespoon organic culinary lavender

½ teaspoon baking powder

1 tablespoon Golden Ghee (page 224)

Grated zest of 1 Meyer lemon

Grass-fed butter

Sugar-free maple syrup

SWEET ANGEL EGGS

SERVES 2 / PREP TIME: 15 MINUTES

4 large free-range eggs, hardboiled and peeled

2 tablespoons mayonnaise

1 tablespoon Sugar-Free Vanilla Bean Sweetener (page 196; optional)

⅛ teaspoon ground cinnamon

RECIPE TIP *If you're in a hurry, use Miracle Whip in place of the mayonnaise and sweetener.*

Deviled eggs . . . my loves . . . my everythings . . . . I always have hardboiled eggs on hand for salads and on-the-go snacks. These breakfast-friendly deviled eggs are slightly sweet and satisfying— like a cinnamon bun.

1. Halve the eggs lengthwise and scoop the yolks into a small bowl. Place the egg white halves on a plate.

2. Add the mayonnaise, sweetener (if using), and cinnamon to the yolks and mash them together.

3. Transfer the yolk mixture to a zipper-top plastic bag and cut off a small corner of the bag at the bottom. Pipe some of the yolk mixture into each egg white half. Serve.

PER SERVING: CALORIES: 184; TOTAL FAT: 15G; SATURATED FAT: 4G; PROTEIN: 12G; CHOLESTEROL: 331MG; CARBOHYDRATES: 1G; FIBER: 0G; **NET CARBS: 1G**

FAT: 72% / CARBS: 2% / PROTEIN: 26%

GARLIC AND THYME BAKED EGG

SERVES 1 / PREP TIME: 10 MINUTES / COOK TIME: 5 MINUTES

Butter and cream form the base of this delicious baked egg. Fragrant rosemary is a wonderful substitute for thyme if you prefer, but, in either case, use fresh herbs, not dried. This recipe takes only a few minutes to make, but you'll be thinking about it all day.

1. Preheat the oven to broil.

2. In a small bowl, mix the garlic, thyme, Parmesan cheese, salt, and a couple of cranks of pepper.

3. Combine the heavy cream and ghee in an 8-ounce ramekin. Place the ramekin on a rimmed baking sheet (for easier transport) and place it under the broiler until it begins to boil, about 1 minute (keep an eye on it as it could take less time).

4. Remove the baking sheet from the oven, and carefully and quickly crack the egg into the ramekin. Just as quickly spoon the herb mixture over the top of the egg. Place the baking sheet back under the broiler until the egg white is opaque, about 3 minutes more.

5. Remove the baked egg from the oven and let it rest and carryover cook for another minute. Serve immediately.

1 garlic clove, minced

Leaves from 1 thyme sprig

1½ teaspoons grated organic Parmesan cheese

Pinch sea salt

Freshly ground black pepper

1 tablespoon organic heavy (whipping) cream

1½ teaspoons Golden Ghee (page 224) or grass-fed butter

1 large free-range egg

MAKE IT PALEO *Increase the ghee to 1½ tablespoons and omit the Parmesan cheese and heavy cream. You'll still end up with a rich, buttery, herbed egg.*

PER SERVING: CALORIES: 182; TOTAL FAT: 17G;
SATURATED FAT: 9G; PROTEIN: 6G; CHOLESTEROL: 203MG;
CARBOHYDRATES: 1G; FIBER: 0G; **NET CARBS: 1G**

FAT: 84% / CARBS: 2% / PROTEIN: 14%

THE BEST FRIED EGGS YOU'LL EVER EAT

SERVES 1 / PREP TIME: 5 MINUTES / COOK TIME: 5 MINUTES

2 pinches onion powder

Pinch ground cumin

Pinch ground coriander

Pinch sweet paprika

Pinch chili powder

Pinch dried parsley

Pinch garlic salt

Pinch sea salt

1½ teaspoons Golden Ghee (page 224)

2 large free-range eggs

RECIPE TIP *If you love this spice mix, turn the "pinches" into tablespoons and store it in an airtight container to use as needed.*

This spice mix adds color and pep to your plate. It goes great over everything, but it especially turns boring eggs into a wow dish. Everyone will want in on your "secret recipe."

1. In a small bowl, combine the onion powder, cumin, coriander, paprika, chili powder, parsley, garlic salt, and sea salt. Set aside.

2. Over medium heat, melt the ghee in a small nonstick skillet.

3. Crack the eggs into the skillet and fry them until the whites are cooked, 3 to 5 minutes. Carefully flip them over (try not to break the yolks) and cook for 10 seconds more.

4. Transfer the eggs to a plate and sprinkle them with the spice mix (save any extra for later).

PER SERVING: CALORIES: 205; TOTAL FAT: 17G;
SATURATED FAT: 7G; PROTEIN: 13G; CHOLESTEROL: 388MG;
CARBOHYDRATES: 2G; FIBER: 0G; **NET CARBS: 2G**

FAT: 75% / CARBS: 2% / PROTEIN: 23%

SPICY PULLED PORK EGGS BENEDICT

SERVES 1 / PREP TIME: 10 MINUTES / COOK TIME: 3 MINUTES

A now-closed restaurant in Providence, Rhode Island, was the only place I willingly ordered eggs Benedict since starting my keto lifestyle. Not because I don't like eggs Benedict, but I felt it would just not be the same without an English muffin or a fresh buttery biscuit. That all changed when I was served a plate full of pulled pork eggs Benedict. Even without the bread, it was still filling and wonderful. But breakfast should be easy, and traditional hollandaise sauce is not. So to make this a quick and easy keto breakfast, I use a delicious microwave hollandaise sauce on top of poached eggs and leftover pulled pork from the previous night's dinner. The combination of savory pulled pork and rich hollandaise sauce is sure to satisfy all morning.

FOR THE HOLLANDAISE SAUCE

2 large free-range egg yolks

2 tablespoons Golden Ghee (page 224), melted

1 teaspoon freshly squeezed Meyer lemon juice

Pinch paprika

Pinch sea salt

Pinch cayenne pepper

TO MAKE THE HOLLANDAISE SAUCE

1. In a small microwave-safe bowl, gently whisk the egg yolks with the ghee, lemon juice, paprika, salt, and cayenne pepper.

2. Microwave the mixture for 20 seconds and then whisk again until the sauce is smooth. Set aside.

»

FOR THE EGGS BENEDICT

1 teaspoon white vinegar

2 large free-range eggs

½ cup Spiced Pulled
Pork (page 167),
heated through

TO MAKE THE EGGS BENEDICT

1. Bring a small pot of water to a simmer. Add the vinegar to the hot water.

2. Crack the eggs into a small bowl, and roll them around lightly so that the whites surround the yolk of the egg. Do not use an egg with a broken yolk.

3. Gently pour the eggs into the simmering water and poach them for 3 minutes.

4. Meanwhile, put the heated pulled pork on a plate.

5. Remove the poached eggs from the water with a slotted spoon and dry them gently with a paper towel. Place the eggs on top of the pulled pork and spoon the hollandaise sauce over the eggs. Serve immediately.

PER SERVING: CALORIES: 569; TOTAL FAT: 47G;
SATURATED FAT: 23G; PROTEIN: 26G; CHOLESTEROL: 882MG;
CARBOHYDRATES: 6G; FIBER: 0G; **NET CARBS: 6G**

FAT: 76% / CARBS: 4% / PROTEIN: 20%

CAJUN CAULIFLOWER AND EGG HASH

SERVES 4 / PREP TIME: 10 MINUTES / COOK TIME: 20 MINUTES

Although cauliflower is keto-friendly, I admit it's not the tastiest vegetable around. But when combined with intense flavors in this breakfast dish—think Cajun seasoning and pastrami scrambled with fresh eggs—I'm a huge fan.

1. Set a steamer rack inside a large pot and pour in just enough water to come to the bottom of the rack. Bring the water to a boil over high heat. Add the cauliflower, cover the pot, and steam the cauliflower until tender, about 6 minutes. Drain the cauliflower and chop it into bite-size pieces. Set aside.

2. In a medium skillet, heat the olive oil over medium heat. Add the onion and sauté it until soft but not browned, 3 to 5 minutes.

3. Add the eggs to the skillet and gently stir to scramble them with the onion, about 2 minutes.

4. Stir the cauliflower, pastrami, green bell pepper, garlic, and Cajun seasoning into the scrambled eggs and onion. Continue cooking the mixture, stirring occasionally, until hot, about 5 minutes more. Serve immediately.

1 (1-pound) bag frozen cauliflower florets

2 tablespoons extra-virgin olive oil

½ sweet yellow onion, chopped

4 large free-range eggs, lightly beaten

8 ounces shaved pastrami, chopped

½ green bell pepper, chopped

2 tablespoons minced garlic

1 teaspoon Cajun seasoning

PER SERVING: CALORIES: 260; TOTAL FAT: 15G;
SATURATED FAT: 4G; PROTEIN: 22G; CHOLESTEROL: 225MG;
CARBOHYDRATES: 10G; FIBER: 4G; **NET CARBS: 6G**

FAT: 54% / CARBS: 10% / PROTEIN: 36%

SCRAMBLED CINNAMON AND CREAM CHEESE EGGS

SERVES 6 / PREP TIME: 10 MINUTES / COOK TIME: 5 MINUTES

6 tablespoons organic cream cheese, at room temperature

2 tablespoons organic heavy (whipping) cream

3 large free-range eggs

1 teaspoon coconut flour

½ teaspoon ground cinnamon

Sweetener

1 tablespoon Golden Ghee (page 224)

Sugar-free maple syrup

These eggs are a complete keto luxury. You get a pancake-like batch of scrambled eggs topped with some of your favorite sugar-free maple syrup. I sometimes even eat these for dessert.

1. In a blender, combine the cream cheese, heavy cream, eggs, coconut flour, cinnamon, and sweetener to taste. Blend until well mixed.

2. In a medium skillet, melt the ghee over medium heat. Pour in the cream cheese and egg mixture. Using a spatula, gently stir the mixture to scramble it until it is cooked through, about 5 minutes.

3. Transfer to a plate and drizzle with your favorite keto-friendly sugar-free maple syrup. Serve immediately.

PER SERVING (WITHOUT SYRUP): CALORIES: 119; TOTAL FAT: 11G; SATURATED FAT: 6G; PROTEIN: 4G; CHOLESTEROL: 110MG; CARBOHYDRATES: 1G; FIBER: 0G; **NET CARBS: 1G**

FAT: 83% / CARBS: 4% / PROTEIN: 13%

HARVEST OMELET

SERVES 1 / PREP TIME: 10 MINUTES / COOK TIME: 20 MINUTES

One lucky morning my husband and I went to break-fast in Portsmouth, Rhode Island, to a cute little diner called Cindy's Country Cafe. I'm not much of a break-fast person; I closed my eyes and pointed to a menu item, hoping it was something I'd like. Turns out I had picked the harvest omelet, and it was the best omelet I've ever had. I attempted to re-create it at home, and this is my version, which I make at least once a week. There's something magical about the flavor of car-amelized onions mixed with sweet, juicy Macintosh apples. That said, feel free to vary this recipe with your favorite keto-friendly ingredients.

1. In a medium skillet, heat 1 teaspoon of olive oil over medium heat. Once the oil is hot, add the sausage links. Cook them, turning frequently, until cooked through, about 5 minutes. Remove the links from the skillet and cut into thin slices. Set aside.

2. Add the onion, apple, and water to the same skillet. Cook over medium heat until soft and caramelized, about 5 minutes. Transfer to a bowl and set aside.

3. In a small skillet, heat the remaining 1 teaspoon of olive oil over medium heat. When the oil is hot, add the egg whites to the pan and let them cook, without stirring, until they are completely opaque. Carefully flip the omelet over, being careful not to break it.

»

2 teaspoons extra-virgin olive oil, divided

4 organic breakfast sausage links

1 tablespoon minced white onion

1 tablespoon minced Macintosh apple

1 tablespoon water

4 large free-range egg whites

½ cup shredded organic Cheddar cheese

Sea salt

Freshly ground black pepper

COOKING TIP *The onion should cook in the water and the juice of the apple, but if it begins to burn before fully caramelizing, add another tablespoon or two of water.*

4. Place the sausage slices evenly over half of the omelet. Spoon the onion and apple mixture over the sausage. Add the Cheddar cheese on top of the onion and apple. Fold the empty half of the omelet over the filled half. Cover the skillet and cook the omelet until the cheese is melted, another 1 to 2 minutes. Season with salt and pepper and serve immediately.

———

PER SERVING: CALORIES: 560; TOTAL FAT: 43G; SATURATED FAT: 18G; PROTEIN: 39G; CHOLESTEROL: 103MG; CARBOHYDRATES: 3G; FIBER: 0G; **NET CARBS: 3G**

FAT: 69% / CARBS: 3% / PROTEIN: 28%

OMELET WITH ASPARAGUS AND SPRING ONIONS

SERVES 2 / PREP TIME: 10 MINUTES / COOK TIME: 20 MINUTES

This light omelet is simple to make but delightfully complex in flavor. It is elevated with asparagus, spring onions, and fresh herbs. The Havarti cheese adds a slightly sharp and buttery layer of flavor.

1 cup 1-inch asparagus pieces

3 large free-range eggs

3 tablespoons organic heavy (whipping) cream

½ teaspoon sea salt

2 tablespoons Golden Ghee (page 224)

1 cup shaved organic Havarti cheese

2 tablespoons chopped fresh thyme leaves

2 tablespoons chopped spring onions

1 tablespoon chopped wild fennel

1. Set a steamer rack inside a large pot and pour in just enough water to come to the bottom of the rack. Bring the water to a boil over high heat. Add the asparagus, cover the pot, and steam the asparagus until tender, about 6 minutes. Drain the asparagus and set aside.

2. In a small bowl, whisk together the eggs, heavy cream, and salt.

3. In a medium skillet, melt the ghee over medium heat, rolling it around the pan as it melts, to coat the surface.

4. Pour the egg mixture into the skillet and let it cook until it can be flipped easily without breaking, about 5 minutes.

5. Once the omelet is flipped, layer the cheese, asparagus, thyme, onions, and fennel over half of the omelet. Continue cooking the omelet until the cheese melts, about 5 minutes more.

6. Fold the empty half of the omelet over the filled half and slide it onto a plate. Serve immediately.

PER SERVING: CALORIES: 528; TOTAL FAT: 46G;
SATURATED FAT: 27G; PROTEIN: 25G; CHOLESTEROL: 1030MG;
CARBOHYDRATES: 5G; FIBER: 2G; **NET CARBS: 3G**

FAT: 78% / CARBS: 2% / PROTEIN: 20%

ROSEMARY QUICHE

SERVES 6 / PREP TIME: 10 MINUTES / COOK TIME: 30 MINUTES

1 teaspoon rosemary-infused olive oil

6 large free-range eggs

½ cup heavy organic (whipping) cream

2 tablespoons organic cream cheese, at room temperature

7 ounces ham, cubed

1 teaspoon fresh rosemary, chopped

1 teaspoon sea salt

RECIPE TIP *If you find a good sliced rosemary ham at your local deli, you can line the bottom of the pie dish with the slices to form a "crust."*

You don't need fancy equipment or ingredients to make a good quiche. The combination of rosemary and ham is a match made in heaven. This quiche is large enough to serve a whole family on the cheap.

1. Preheat the oven to 375°F.
2. Rub a shallow 9-inch pie dish with the rosemary olive oil.
3. In a medium bowl, lightly beat the eggs. Stir in the heavy cream, cream cheese, ham, rosemary, and salt. Mix well.
4. Pour the egg mixture into the pie dish and bake until the eggs are set and the top is golden brown, about 30 minutes. Let the quiche rest for at least 10 minutes before serving.

PER SERVING: CALORIES: 184; TOTAL FAT: 14G; SATURATED FAT: 6G; PROTEIN: 12G; CHOLESTEROL: 224MG; CARBOHYDRATES: 2G; FIBER: 1G; **NET CARBS: 1G**

FAT: 69% / CARBS: 4% / PROTEIN: 27%

BREAKFAST TACOS

SERVES 2 / PREP TIME: 10 MINUTES / COOK TIME: 25 MINUTES

Without a tortilla, breakfast burritos are really just scrambled eggs with some taco spices, right? Wrong! Making keto taco "shells" is easy peasy, and their cheesy crunch goes perfect with eggs. The avocado adds luscious flavor and velvety texture to this dish. You won't even miss the sour cream.

1. In a medium bowl, whisk together the eggs, heavy cream, and taco seasoning. Set aside.

2. To make the taco "shells," grease a nonstick skillet with olive oil and place it over medium heat. Once the oil is hot, put ½ cup of cheese in the middle of the skillet, making a circle of cheese about 4 inches in diameter. Cook the cheese until it is bubbling and starts to brown ever so slightly, 3 to 5 minutes. Remove it from the skillet and form it into a taco shell shape. Stand it upside down to cool. Repeat this process to create 3 more taco shells.

3. Wipe out the skillet, then place it back over medium heat and add the ghee. Once melted, give the egg mixture a quick stir and add it to the skillet. Gently stir the eggs until scrambled and cooked through, about 5 minutes.

4. To serve, divide the eggs between the taco "shells" and top with the avocado slices and a dash of cayenne pepper sauce.

3 large free-range eggs

2 tablespoons organic heavy (whipping) cream

1 tablespoon Golden Taco Seasoning (page 217)

Extra-virgin olive oil

2 cups shredded organic Mexican cheese blend, divided

1 tablespoon Golden Ghee (page 224)

1 avocado, peeled, pitted, and sliced

Cayenne pepper sauce

MAKE IT PALEO *Scrambled eggs don't require cream—it just makes them fluffier. Use 1 tablespoon of unsweetened almond milk in its place.*

PER SERVING: CALORIES: 895; TOTAL FAT: 79G;
SATURATED FAT: 38G; PROTEIN: 40G; CHOLESTEROL: 435MG;
CARBOHYDRATES: 8G; FIBER: 7G; **NET CARBS: 1G**

FAT: 79% / CARBS: 3% / PROTEIN: 18%

JERK BACON

SERVES 4 / PREP TIME: 5 MINUTES / COOK TIME: 20 MINUTES

1 pound uncured center-cut bacon (as thick-cut as you can get)

2 pinches cayenne pepper

2 pinches onion powder

2 pinches dried thyme

2 pinches coconut sugar

Pinch smoked paprika

Pinch ground ginger

Pinch ground allspice

Pinch ground nutmeg

Pinch ground cinnamon

Pinch garlic powder

Pinch coarsely ground black pepper

Pinch red pepper flakes

Since trying the various bacons—spicy, chocolate, candied, lavender, among others—made by a wonderful Charlottesville, Virginia, restaurant, I haven't been able to eat bacon straight up since. This is my all-time favorite recipe for kicking breakfast bacon up a notch.

1. Preheat the oven to 400°F.
2. Line two rimmed baking sheets with parchment paper.
3. Place the bacon strips in a single layer on the sheets.
4. In a small bowl, mix all the seasonings. Sprinkle this mixture over the bacon strips.
5. Bake the bacon to your desired crispiness, 15 to 20 minutes (no need to flip the bacon midbake).
6. Remove the bacon from the oven and let it cool for a few minutes before serving.

PER SERVING: CALORIES: 240; TOTAL FAT: 24G; SATURATED FAT: 8G; PROTEIN: 4G; CHOLESTEROL: 20MG; CARBOHYDRATES: 0G; FIBER: 0G; **NET CARBS: 0G**

FAT: 70% / CARBS: 3% / PROTEIN: 27%

MORNING MEATLOAF

SERVES 4 / PREP TIME: 10 MINUTES / COOK TIME: 35 MINUTES

Mornings are better with meat. Here, onions and scallion are balanced with plenty of cheese. The best part: make this on Sunday and it will last you all week long for quick and easy breakfasts.

1. Preheat the oven to 350°F.

2. Grease a small loaf pan with some ghee.

3. In a large bowl, lightly beat the eggs. Add the sausage, onion, and half of the cream cheese. Mix thoroughly.

4. Pour the meatloaf and egg mixture into the loaf pan. Place in the oven and bake, uncovered, for about 30 minutes.

5. Remove the meatloaf from the oven and let sit for 5 minutes. Use a spoon to lightly scrape off any fat that may have risen to the top. Spread the remaining cream cheese over the top of the meatloaf, and top it with Cheddar cheese and scallions.

6. Bake the meatloaf for about 5 more minutes, then switch to broil for about 3 minutes, until the Cheddar cheese begins to turn golden and crisp. Remove the meatloaf from the oven and let sit for at least 5 minutes before slicing and serving.

Golden Ghee (page 224)

6 large free-range eggs

1 pound bulk sausage (like Jimmy Dean)

¼ yellow onion, chopped

4 ounces organic cream cheese, at room temperature, divided

1 cup shredded organic Cheddar cheese

2 tablespoons chopped scallion

PER SERVING: CALORIES: 682; TOTAL FAT: 56G;
SATURATED FAT: 24G; PROTEIN: 38G; CHOLESTEROL: 426MG;
CARBOHYDRATES: 5G; FIBER: 0.5G; **NET CARBS: 4.5G**

FAT: 74% / CARBS: 3% / PROTEIN: 23%

CHAPTER THREE

DRINKS, SHAKES & SMOOTHIES

LEMON-MINT ICE CUBES

SERVES 12 / PREP TIME: 5 MINUTES, PLUS FREEZING TIME

4 large mint leaves, chopped

½ cucumber, quartered lengthwise and sliced crosswise

1 cup freshly squeezed lemon juice

1 cup water

I don't know about you, but I'm the worst at meeting any kind of water quota for the day. There are times when I realize before bed that I haven't had even a single cup of water all day. On keto, as with any diet, it's important to drink a lot of water to keep your body flushed and your digestion on par. I find that adding these mojito-esque ice cubes to infusion pitchers or to glasses of water makes it easier for me to reach my hydration goals.

1. Distribute the mint leaves and cucumbers evenly in an ice cube tray.
2. Fill each cube halfway with lemon juice and the rest of the way with water.
3. Freeze, then pop out each ice cube as needed.

PER SERVING: CALORIES: 7; TOTAL FAT: 0G; SATURATED FAT: 0G; PROTEIN: 0G; CHOLESTEROL: 0MG; CARBOHYDRATES: 1G; FIBER: 0G; **NET CARBS: 1G**

FAT: 0% / CARBS: 100% / PROTEIN: 0%

STRAWBERRY-LIME WATER

SERVES 6 TO 8 / PREP TIME: 5 MINUTES, PLUS 1 HOUR TO INFUSE

Of all the water infusions out there, this is my favorite. The lime makes you want to drink more and supposedly helps alkalize you, while strawberries add a light sweetness that complements the lime perfectly.

1. Pour the water into an infusion pitcher.

2. Add the lime and strawberry slices to the water.

3. Let the water infuse for at least 1 hour in the refrigerator and drink within 2 days.

2 quarts water

1 lime, cut into ⅛-inch-thick wheels

5 large strawberries, hulled and sliced

PER SERVING: CALORIES: 4; TOTAL FAT: 0G;
SATURATED FAT: 0G; PROTEIN: 0G; CHOLESTEROL: 0MG;
CARBOHYDRATES: 1G; FIBER: 0G; **NET CARBS: 1G**

FAT: 0% / CARBS: 100% / PROTEIN: 0%

COCONUT GREEN TEA

SERVES 1 / PREP TIME: 5 MINUTES

1 green tea bag

1 cup hot water

1 tablespoon coconut oil

KETO TIP *Green tea is rich in L-theanine, which counteracts anxiety and eases the jittery effects of other caffeinated products. L-theanine also increases dopamine, along with the production of alpha waves, to restore balance to your mind and body.*

I always drink green tea with coconut oil in it. The coconut eliminates the bitterness in the tea and adds a dose of healthy fatty acids.

1. Steep the green tea in the hot water for 3 minutes.
2. Remove the tea bag and pour the hot tea into a single-serving blender with the coconut oil. Blend briefly to mix and pour back into the tea mug.

PER SERVING: CALORIES: 121; TOTAL FAT: 13G; SATURATED FAT: 11G; PROTEIN: 0G; CHOLESTEROL: 0MG; CARBOHYDRATES: 0G; FIBER: 0G; **NET CARBS: 0G**

FAT: 100% / CARBS: 0% / PROTEIN: 0%

EARL GREY HOT CHOCOLATE

SERVES 1 / PREP TIME: 5 MINUTES / COOK TIME: 10 MINUTES

Don't tread on my hot chocolate parade: this is the best recipe that exists for ketogenic hot chocolate and I won't hear anything else. When I spent a couple of weeks in New Orleans, I was introduced to the London Fog—Earl Grey tea with cream, vanilla, and honey—and it blew my socks off. Sure, my cup had RumChata in it, which may have added to the splendor, but now, every time I smell Earl Grey I swear I can hear the distant sound of jazz at Maison Bourbon.

1. In a small pot, bring the almond milk to a steaming simmer over medium heat. Stir in the chocolate until it is dissolved completely and smooth, about 3 minutes.

2. Pour the hot chocolate into a mug and stir in the heavy cream. Add the tea bag to the mug and steep it for 5 minutes. Remove the tea bag and enjoy.

PER SERVING: CALORIES: 145; TOTAL FAT: 13G;
SATURATED FAT: 7G; PROTEIN: 2G; CHOLESTEROL: 24MG;
CARBOHYDRATES: 7G; FIBER: 2G; **NET CARBS: 5G**

FAT: 81% / CARBS: 14% / PROTEIN: 5%

1 cup unsweetened almond milk

½ ounce organic dark chocolate (at least 73% cacao)

1 tablespoon organic heavy (whipping) cream

1 Earl Grey tea bag

KETO TIP *High-quality organic chocolate is less likely to include fillers, and you can find organic cacao blends that are naturally low carb. Skip sugar-free chocolate, as it's full of ingredients you can't pronounce.*

BUTTER-CINNAMON COFFEE

SERVES 1 / PREP TIME: 5 MINUTES

1 cup hot brewed coffee

1 tablespoon unsalted grass-fed butter

⅛ teaspoon ground cinnamon

MAKE IT PALEO *Replace the butter with 1½ teaspoons of coconut oil.*

This is a must for any ketoer. Cinnamon serves as a natural sweetener in coffee, and butter adds a level of creaminess and healthy fats, although you can add cream if you want.

In a single-serving blender, combine the coffee, butter, and cinnamon. Blend until smooth. Pour into a mug and enjoy.

PER SERVING: CALORIES: 108; TOTAL FAT: 12G; SATURATED FAT: 7G; PROTEIN: 0G; CHOLESTEROL: 21MG; CARBOHYDRATES: 0G; FIBER: 0G; **NET CARBS: 0G**

FAT: 100% / CARBS: 0% / PROTEIN: 0%

FROZEN COFFEE SHAKE

SERVES 1 / PREP TIME: 5 MINUTES

In the Northeast, summer memories collide with daily doses of frozen coffee, which you can find at just about any coffee shop. Why not make your own?

1. In a blender, combine the coffee, heavy cream, sweetener, and ice cubes. Blend until smooth.

2. Pour into a mug or glass and top with the whipped cream.

PER SERVING: CALORIES: 488; TOTAL FAT: 52G; SATURATED FAT: 32G; PROTEIN: 3G; CHOLESTEROL: 190MG; CARBOHYDRATES: 0G; FIBER: 0G; **NET CARBS: 0G**

FAT: 95% / CARBS: 0% / PROTEIN: 5%

1 cup cold brewed coffee

⅓ cup organic heavy (whipping) cream

2 tablespoons Sugar-Free Vanilla Bean Sweetener (page 196)

7 ice cubes

½ cup Whipped Cream (page 197)

CHOCOLATE-RASPBERRY CHEESECAKE SHAKE

SERVES 1 / PREP TIME: 5 MINUTES

1 cup unsweetened almond milk

1 tablespoon organic heavy (whipping) cream

1 tablespoon organic cream cheese, at room temperature

⅓ cup low-carb vanilla or graham cracker whey protein powder

½ cup raspberries

2 ice cubes

If cheesecake is your weakness, why not drink it too? This shake includes all the luxurious ingredients of a cheesecake, whipped up into a frothy, straw-worthy drink.

In a blender, combine the almond milk, heavy cream, cream cheese, protein powder, raspberries, and ice cubes. Blend until smooth and then pour into a tall glass to serve.

PER SERVING: CALORIES: 251; TOTAL FAT: 15G; SATURATED FAT: 6G; PROTEIN: 25G; CHOLESTEROL: 87MG; CARBOHYDRATES: 9G; FIBER: 5G; **NET CARBS: 4G**

FAT: 54% / CARBS: 6% / PROTEIN: 40%

CHOCOLATE–PEANUT BUTTER SMOOTHIE

SERVES 1 / PREP TIME: 5 MINUTES

This shake tastes like the first bite of one of those chocolaty, peanut buttery candy bites I savored as a kid after a long night of Halloween trick-or-treating.

In a blender, combine the water, heavy cream, protein powder, ice cubes, and peanut butter. Blend until smooth and then pour into a tall glass to serve.

———

PER SERVING: CALORIES: 604; TOTAL FAT: 49G; SATURATED FAT: 24G; PROTEIN: 33G; CHOLESTEROL: 124MG; CARBOHYDRATES: 8G; FIBER: 2G; **NET CARBS: 6G**

FAT: 73% / CARBS: 4% / PROTEIN: 23%

1 cup water

⅓ cup organic heavy (whipping) cream

⅓ cup low-carb chocolate whey protein powder

2 ice cubes

2 tablespoons peanut butter

STRAWBERRY-SAGE SMOOTHIE

SERVES 1 / PREP TIME: 5 MINUTES

1 cup unsweetened coconut milk

2 tablespoons organic heavy (whipping) cream

5 frozen strawberries

1 fresh sage leaf

1 teaspoon Sugar-Free Vanilla Bean Sweetener (page 196; optional)

While some keto purists may snub their noses at berries, keto can be more satisfying in a dietary balance when you look at it as the process of staying in ketosis and not restricting everything and anything with carbs. Never in my keto life have I been kicked out of ketosis by a handful of berries. Enjoy this sweet, tart, and slightly savory strawberry cocktail without guilt, and see how much more your taste buds appreciate sweet strawberries now that you've removed most sugars from your diet.

In a blender, combine the coconut milk, heavy cream, strawberries, sage, and sweetener. Blend until smooth and then pour into a tall glass to serve.

———

PER SERVING: CALORIES: 173; TOTAL FAT: 16G; SATURATED FAT: 12G; PROTEIN: 2G; CHOLESTEROL: 41MG; CARBOHYDRATES: 6G; FIBER: 1G; **NET CARBS: 5G**

FAT: 83% / CARBS: 12% / PROTEIN: 5%

CHOCOLATE-COVERED STRAWBERRY SMOOTHIE

SERVES 1 / PREP TIME: 5 MINUTES

Strawberries dipped in chocolate aren't just for special occasions. They make an indulgent treat for breakfast on any keto-rific morning.

In a blender, combine the water, heavy cream, protein powder, and strawberries. Blend until smooth and then pour into a tall glass to serve.

PER SERVING: CALORIES: 273; TOTAL FAT: 17G;
SATURATED FAT: 10G; PROTEIN: 24G; CHOLESTEROL: 67MG;
CARBOHYDRATES: 4G; FIBER: 1G; **NET CARBS: 3G**

FAT: 58% / CARBS: 4% / PROTEIN: 38%

1 cup water

3 tablespoons organic heavy (whipping) cream

⅓ cup low-carb chocolate whey protein powder

3 frozen strawberries

GINGER-BASIL AVOCADO SMOOTHIE

SERVES 1 / PREP TIME: 5 MINUTES

½ avocado, chopped

⅓ cup low-carb vanilla whey protein powder

½ teaspoon grated fresh ginger

1 tablespoon chopped fresh basil

1 cup unsweetened almond milk

2 ice cubes

The trouble with smoothies is that they're typically lacking in the fat department, making them delicious but not exactly fueling our energy while in ketosis. The solution? Throw avocado into any smoothie for some good, healthy, filling fats.

In a blender, combine the avocado, protein powder, ginger, basil, almond milk, and ice cubes. Blend until smooth and then pour into a tall glass to serve.

PER SERVING: CALORIES: 343; TOTAL FAT: 22G;
SATURATED FAT: 5G; PROTEIN: 25G; CHOLESTEROL: 55MG;
CARBOHYDRATES: 12G; FIBER: 8G; **NET CARBS: 4G**

FAT: 61% / CARBS: 11% / PROTEIN: 28%

MEXICAN CHOCOLATE SMOOTHIE

SERVES 1 / PREP TIME: 5 MINUTES

One cold afternoon in Boston, I took a tour of the Taza Chocolate factory and got to try their many stone-ground chocolates. You've probably seen those big, round discs of Taza chocolate at natural food stores, cafés, and bookshops. (I totally get the appeal of chocolate and books, by the way.) One of their flavors is a Mexican chocolate, which I didn't quite under-stand at the time, as it's flavored with cayenne pepper. Years after the tour I tried it in Seattle, remembering my spicy nibbles years before. Ever since, whenever I see Mexican hot chocolate, I lose my mind a little and feel the need to tell everyone, "Mexican chocolate is sooooo good, you guys." And like the hot version, this spicy cold edition is sooooo good. And cayenne pep-per is also sooooo good for you—it aids in digestion, stimulates circulation, and supports weight loss just to name a few benefits.

In a blender, combine the almond milk, heavy cream, protein powder, cinnamon, cayenne pepper, and ice cubes. Blend until smooth and then pour into a tall glass to serve.

———

PER SERVING: CALORIES: 193; TOTAL FAT: 10G;
SATURATED FAT: 5G; PROTEIN: 23G; CHOLESTEROL: 76MG;
CARBOHYDRATES: 3G; FIBER: 1G; **NET CARBS: 2G**

FAT: 47% / CARBS: 4% / PROTEIN: 49%

1 cup unsweetened almond milk

1 tablespoon organic heavy (whipping) cream

⅓ cup low-carb chocolate whey protein powder

¼ teaspoon ground cinnamon

Pinch cayenne pepper

2 ice cubes

SALTED CHOCOLATE AND MACADAMIA NUT SMOOTHIE

SERVES 1 / PREP TIME: 5 MINUTES

1 cup unsweetened
almond milk

⅓ cup low-carb chocolate
whey protein powder

2 tablespoons salted
macadamia nuts

Macadamia nuts have carbs but are also high in fat and fiber, which balances out and makes them a great keto snack. Because of the carbs, though, I like to pair them with the always-trusty unsweetened almond milk.

In a blender, combine the almond milk, protein powder, and macadamias. Blend until smooth and then pour into a tall glass to serve.

PER SERVING: CALORIES: 165; TOTAL FAT: 12G;
SATURATED FAT: 2G; PROTEIN: 12G; CHOLESTEROL: 20MG;
CARBOHYDRATES: 4G; FIBER: 3G; **NET CARBS: 1G**

FAT: 68% / CARBS: 2% / PROTEIN: 30%

ALMOND MILK EGGNOG

SERVES 1 / PREP TIME: 5 MINUTES / COOK TIME: 15 MINUTES, PLUS 3 HOURS TO CHILL

This eggnog will be on your forever list of go-to drinks. It's rich and creamy and tastes like custard. I often make this at night so that it's ready for breakfast.

1. In a single-serving blender, combine the eggs, almond milk, sweetener, vanilla bean seeds, cinnamon, and nutmeg. Blend until smooth.

2. Transfer the mixture to a small saucepan and heat it over medium-low heat until thick, about 15 minutes, stirring frequently.

3. Cover the pan and refrigerate it for at least 3 hours, or overnight.

4. Fold the whipped cream into the eggnog and pour it into a glass to serve.

PER SERVING: CALORIES: 262; TOTAL FAT: 22G; SATURATED FAT: 10G; PROTEIN: 16G; CHOLESTEROL: 368MG; CARBOHYDRATES: 1G; FIBER: 1G; **NET CARBS: 0G**

FAT: 75% / CARBS: 0% / PROTEIN: 25%

2 large free-range eggs

1 cup unsweetened almond milk

2 tablespoons Sugar-Free Vanilla Bean Sweetener (page 196)

Pinch vanilla bean seeds

Pinch ground cinnamon

Pinch ground nutmeg

¼ cup unsweetened Whipped Cream (page 197)

COOKING TIP *If the eggs begin to scramble while on the heat, just keep stirring the mixture. Then, when it's done cooking, pour it back into the blender and blend until smooth. It will be slightly thicker but still delicious.*

SNACKS

PORK RIND NACHOS

1 medium tomato, seeded and chopped

¼ white onion, chopped

1 tablespoon chopped fresh cilantro

1 jalapeño pepper, seeded and minced

1 teaspoon minced garlic

1½ teaspoons freshly squeezed lime juice

Sea salt

Freshly ground black pepper

1 (1½-ounce) bag pork rinds

2 cups shredded organic Cheddar cheese

Nachos, my first love, my last love. While a pork rind can never truly replace a tortilla chip, the more toppings you add, the less you'll care which vehicle is driving all that delicious cheese into your mouth.

1. In a small bowl, toss together the tomato, onion, cilantro, jalapeño, and garlic. Stir in the lime juice and then season with salt and pepper. Set the salsa aside for at least 1 hour for the flavors to combine. After 1 hour, drain any excess liquid from the salsa.

2. Preheat the oven to 350°F.

3. Line a rimmed baking sheet with parchment paper or aluminum foil.

4. Spread out the pork rinds in a tight but single layer on the sheet. Sprinkle the cheese over the pork rinds, then top with the salsa.

5. Bake the nachos until the cheese melts and begins to bubble, about 15 minutes. Transfer to a platter and serve hot.

PER SERVING: CALORIES: 599; TOTAL FAT: 45G; SATURATED FAT: 26G; PROTEIN: 41G; CHOLESTEROL: 149MG; CARBOHYDRATES: 6G; FIBER: 1G; **NET CARBS: 5G**

FAT: 68% / CARBS: 5% / PROTEIN: 27%

SOUR CREAM AND ONION PORK RINDS

SERVES 4 TO 6 / PREP TIME: 20 MINUTES / COOK TIME: 2½ HOURS

Pork rinds have this amazing ability to take on the flavor of whatever you spice them with, making these a crave-worthy sour cream and onion "chip." You can usually get pork skin from a butcher or at your local international market; otherwise you can purchase "pork rind pellets" online.

1. Preheat the oven to 350°F.

2. Line a rimmed baking sheet with parchment paper.

3. Using kitchen shears, cut the pork skin into 1-inch squares and place each square skin-side up on the sheet.

4. Bake the skins for 2½ hours. Remove the baking sheet from the oven and set aside until the pork rinds are cool enough to handle.

5. In a large bowl, toss the warm pork rinds with the chives, buttermilk powder, onion powder, and garlic powder. Serve warm or at room temperature.

2 pounds pork skin

3 tablespoons dried chives

3 tablespoons sweet cream buttermilk powder

2 tablespoons onion powder

1 tablespoon garlic powder

KETO TIP *Bob's Red Mill sweet cream buttermilk powder has significantly fewer carbs than other buttermilk powders, giving this recipe a total of 1.5 net carbs, whereas regular buttermilk can range from 3 to 10 net carbs on its own.*

PER SERVING: CALORIES: 278; TOTAL FAT: 19G;
SATURATED FAT: 10G; PROTEIN: 25G; CHOLESTEROL: 90MG;
CARBOHYDRATES: 1.5G; FIBER: 0G; **NET CARBS: 1.5G**

FAT: 62% / CARBS: 2% / PROTEIN: 36%

BAKED CHEDDAR CHIPS

SERVES 4 / PREP TIME: 5 MINUTES / COOK TIME: 5 MINUTES

4 cups shredded organic Cheddar cheese

Sea salt

RECIPE TIP *To take these chips to the next level, mix equal parts chili powder, garlic powder, smoked paprika, and sea salt with three times as much Cheddar cheese powder or grated Parmesan cheese. Sprinkle over the warm cheese.*

These Cheddar chips will satisfy any chip cravings you have, but they work especially well with Mexican dips like salsa and guacamole.

1. Preheat the oven to 350°F.

2. Line a rimmed baking sheet with parchment paper.

3. Spread out the cheese evenly on the sheet.

4. Bake for 3 to 5 minutes, checking regularly until the cheese browns but does not burn.

5. Remove the baking sheet from the oven and season the cheese with salt.

6. While the cheese is still warm, use a pizza cutter to cut it into strips or triangles. Let cool before serving.

PER SERVING: CALORIES: 457; TOTAL FAT: 38G; SATURATED FAT: 24G; PROTEIN: 28G; CHOLESTEROL: 119MG; CARBOHYDRATES: 1G; FIBER: 0G; **NET CARBS: 1G**

FAT: 74% / CARBS: 1% / PROTEIN: 25%

BAKED PARMESAN CHIPS

SERVES 4 / PREP TIME: 5 MINUTES / COOK TIME: 5 MINUTES

These Parmesan chips complement the flavors of just about anything savory you want to put on them or dip them in. They go especially well with the Creamy Crab Dip (page 76).

10 ounces shredded organic Parmesan cheese

Sea salt

1. Preheat the oven to 350°F.

2. Line a rimmed baking sheet with parchment paper.

3. Form small Parmesan cheese circles on the sheet.

4. Bake, checking frequently, until the cheese browns but does not burn, 3 to 5 minutes.

5. Remove from the oven and sprinkle the cheese with the salt. Let cool before serving.

PER SERVING: CALORIES: 228; TOTAL FAT: 15G; SATURATED FAT: 10G; PROTEIN: 23G; CHOLESTEROL: 51MG; CARBOHYDRATES: 2G; FIBER: 0G; **NET CARBS: 2G**

FAT: 58% / CARBS: 2% / PROTEIN: 40%

EVERYTHING PRETZELS

SERVES 1 / PREP TIME: 20 MINUTES / COOK TIME: 15 MINUTES

FOR THE TOPPING

1 teaspoon pretzel
salt or sea salt

½ teaspoon poppy seeds

½ teaspoon sesame seeds

½ teaspoon onion flakes

½ teaspoon garlic flakes

FOR THE PRETZELS

1 tablespoon Golden Ghee
(page 224), melted, plus
additional for brushing

½ cup shredded
low-moisture organic
mozzarella cheese

3 tablespoons
almond flour

½ teaspoon sea salt

¼ teaspoon garlic powder

1 large free-range
egg, lightly beaten

Mustard, for dipping
(optional)

One thing I've learned for sure is that keto cakes can be made from eggs and keto breads can be made from cheese. There's really nothing you can't do with eggs or cheese plus a little almond or coconut flour if you're craving a bread-like treat. Huge props to UpLateAnyway.com, who inspired the dough for this recipe with her famous low-carb stromboli recipe, which, to me, makes her a ketogenic hero.

TO MAKE THE TOPPING

In a small bowl, mix the salt, poppy seeds, sesame seeds, onion flakes, and garlic flakes. Set aside.

TO MAKE THE PRETZELS

1. Preheat the oven to 400°F.

2. In a small microwave-safe bowl, combine the ghee and mozzarella. Microwave on high in 30-second intervals until the mozzarella is melted and you can easily handle it with your hands and roll it into a ball.

3. Add the almond flour, salt, and garlic powder to the mozzarella and stir to combine, and then mix in the egg. If the mixture won't combine like a dough, microwave it in 10-second intervals until it does.

4. Lay out a sheet of parchment paper. Use your hands to roll the dough on the parchment into a long rope about ½ inch in diameter.

5. Cut the dough rope into 6 pieces and form each into a pretzel. Transfer the parchment with the pretzels to a rimmed baking sheet.

6. Brush each pretzel with melted ghee, and then sprinkle each with the topping.

7. Bake for 15 minutes. Serve with a small cup of mustard for dipping (if using).

PER SERVING: CALORIES: 498; TOTAL FAT: 40G; SATURATED FAT: 16G; PROTEIN: 23G; CHOLESTEROL: 227MG; CARBOHYDRATES: 8G; FIBER: 3G; **NET CARBS: 5G**

FAT: 77% / CARBS: 5% / PROTEIN: 18%

MINI MOZZARELLA STICKS

SERVES 4 / PREP TIME: 10 MINUTES, PLUS 1 HOUR TO FREEZE / COOK TIME: 2 MINUTES

1 (1½-ounce) bag
pork rinds

1 tablespoon Italian
seasoning

1 teaspoon garlic powder

¼ teaspoon sea salt

¼ teaspoon freshly
ground black pepper

¼ cup grated organic
Parmesan cheese

1 large free-range egg

1 large free-range
egg white

10 whole-milk organic
mozzarella cheese sticks

Oil, for frying

Marinara sauce, for
dipping (optional)

COOKING TIP *To bake the
mozzarella sticks, don't
freeze them first. Simply bake
at 350°F for about 6 minutes.*

*There's nothing like a crispy, salty, ooey-gooey moz-
zarella stick. The secret to making them is that you
absolutely must make and freeze them in advance;
or they'll end up a hot, ooey-gooey mess all over the
baking sheet instead of in your mouth.*

1. Line a rimmed baking sheet or large plate with
   parchment paper.

2. In a food processor or blender, combine the pork
   rinds, Italian seasoning, garlic powder, salt, and
   pepper. Pulse until you have a bread crumb–like
   consistency. Use a spatula to stir in the Parmesan
   cheese. Transfer some of the mixture to a small bowl.

3. In another small bowl, whisk together the egg and
   egg white.

4. Cut each mozzarella stick into two short halves.

5. Dip each mozzarella half into the egg mixture, then
   roll it in the "breading," refilling the breading as
   needed. Place the coated mozzarella sticks on the
   lined baking sheet or plate.

6. Freeze the mozzarella sticks for at least 1 hour.

7. In a large skillet over medium-high heat, heat
   enough oil to cover the bottom of the pan. When
   the oil is hot, fry the mozzarella sticks for about
   1 minute on each side. Serve warm, with marinara
   sauce for dipping (if using).

PER SERVING: CALORIES: 430; TOTAL FAT: 36G;
SATURATED FAT: 14G; PROTEIN: 29G; CHOLESTEROL: 114MG;
CARBOHYDRATES: 2G; FIBER: 0G; **NET CARBS: 2G**

FAT: 69% / CARBS: 2% / PROTEIN: 29%

MOZZARELLA CRUST PIZZA

SERVES 2 / PREP TIME: 5 MINUTES / COOK TIME: 15 MINUTES

Consider your pizza cravings gone, with this fat-centric pizza where the mozzarella crisps on the bottom and can be cut (and held) like a real pizza. Plus, you'll still get all that classic pizza flavor you crave.

1. Preheat the oven to 400°F.

2. Line a rimmed baking sheet with parchment paper (don't use aluminum foil). Arrange the mozzarella on the sheet in an even layer to form a large rectangle with no holes. Sprinkle the garlic powder and a pinch of pizza seasoning over the cheese. Bake until the cheese is melted and browned all around the edges, 12 to 15 minutes.

3. Remove the baking sheet from the oven and set aside to cool for 3 minutes.

4. Spread the tomato sauce over the top of the crust, and then sprinkle it with the Parmesan cheese and the remaining 1 teaspoon of pizza seasoning. Return the pizza to the oven for about 1 minute. Slice and serve hot.

PER SERVING: CALORIES: 324; TOTAL FAT: 20G;
SATURATED FAT: 12G; PROTEIN: 33G; CHOLESTEROL: 60MG;
CARBOHYDRATES: 4G; FIBER: 1G; **NET CARBS: 3G**

FAT: 55% / CARBS: 4% / PROTEIN: 41%

2 cups shredded organic mozzarella cheese

1 teaspoon garlic powder

1 teaspoon plus a pinch pizza seasoning, divided

½ cup tomato sauce

Grated organic Parmesan cheese

RECIPE TIP *You can use this basic recipe to make any kind of pizza you like. I love to add sausage and banana peppers and place it under the broiler for a few extra minutes, watching carefully so it doesn't burn.*

MINI SALAMI AND CHEESE PIZZAS

SERVES 1 / PREP TIME: 5 MINUTES / COOK TIME: 1 MINUTE

4 slices Genoa salami

4 tablespoons Rhode Island Red Marinara Sauce (page 221), divided

4 tablespoons shredded organic mozzarella cheese, divided

Pizza seasoning

RECIPE TIP *Genoa salami makes this taste like a pepperoni pizza, but you could also use pepperoni slices as the base (for mini-mini pizzas), or find those teeny-tiny pepperoni "dots" and scatter them on top of the cheese.*

Genoa salami slices, smaller than bologna slices but larger than pepperoni, make great low-carb "crusts" for easy mini pizzas you can make in the oven, microwave, or toaster oven. Even your non-keto pals will enjoy these.

1. Preheat the oven to broil.
2. Line a rimmed baking sheet with parchment paper.
3. Lay out the salami slices on the sheet, with space between each one. Top each with 1 tablespoon of marinara. Then sprinkle 1 tablespoon of mozzarella on each pizza and add a pinch of pizza seasoning.
4. Place the pizzas under the broiler until the cheese bubbles, about 1 minute. Serve.

PER SERVING: CALORIES: 259; TOTAL FAT: 19G; SATURATED FAT: 8G; PROTEIN: 17G; CHOLESTEROL: 53MG; CARBOHYDRATES: 4G; FIBER: 1G; **NET CARBS: 3G**

FAT: 66% / CARBS: 5% / PROTEIN: 29%

CHICKEN RAMEN DIP

SERVES 4 TO 6 / PREP TIME: 5 MINUTES, PLUS 1 HOUR TO CHILL

In college, I was not just a ramen girl—I was the ramen girl. I ran a column of ramen recipes on my dorm website and ate ramen just about every day. When a ramen cookbook came out, three people gave it to me for Christmas. I know ramen. I love ramen. I still buy spicy ramen, toss the noodles, and use the seasoning packet to make broth. When I first made this dip, I thought I was just being crazy and projecting like a true ramen addict. But ramen is back and can be enjoyed with fresh veggies or pork rinds. You'll be amazed by how much flavor is packed into each bite.

In a medium bowl, place the sour cream, cream cheese, mayonnaise, and seasoning. With a hand mixer or immersion blender, blend everything until well combined. Cover the bowl and refrigerate the dip for at least 1 hour, or overnight, for the flavors to meld.

6 ounces organic sour cream

¼ cup organic cream cheese, at room temperature

2 tablespoons mayonnaise

1 seasoning packet from a package of chicken ramen or spicy ramen

KETO TIP *Look for 99-cent ramen packages at your supermarket. The noodles aren't keto-friendly, but those seasoning packets are what you're looking for.*

PER SERVING: CALORIES: 156; TOTAL FAT: 16G; SATURATED FAT: 9G; PROTEIN: 3G; CHOLESTEROL: 36MG; CARBOHYDRATES: 1G; FIBER: 0G; **NET CARBS: 1G**

FAT: 90% / CARBS: 3% / PROTEIN: 7%

CREAMY CRAB DIP

SERVES 4 TO 6 / PREP TIME: 10 MINUTES / COOK TIME: 30 MINUTES

Grass-fed butter, at room temperature

1 pound lump crabmeat

½ cup diced red bell pepper

1 cup organic cream cheese, at room temperature

1 tablespoon mayonnaise

1 tablespoon horseradish

2 teaspoons Cajun seasoning

⅛ teaspoon garlic salt

This rich, creamy dip is an homage to the first crab dip I ever had. I snagged every keto-friendly veggie stick and cheese slice to consume scoop after scoop of dip. Ever since, crab dip has been a favorite. This dip goes great with Baked Parmesan Chips (page 69).

1. Preheat the oven to 350°F.
2. Grease a small baking dish with butter.
3. In a medium bowl, mix the crabmeat, red bell pepper, cream cheese, mayonnaise, horseradish, Cajun seasoning, and garlic salt until well blended.
4. Transfer the dip to the baking dish and bake for 30 minutes. Serve warm.

PER SERVING: CALORIES: 292; TOTAL FAT: 31G; SATURATED FAT: 13G; PROTEIN: 21G; CHOLESTEROL: 129MG; CARBOHYDRATES: 2G; FIBER: 0G; **NET CARBS: 2G**

FAT: 67% / CARBS: 3% / PROTEIN: 30%

BACON-WHISKEY CARAMELIZED ONION DIP

SERVES 4 TO 6 / PREP TIME: 10 MINUTES, PLUS 2 HOURS TO CHILL / COOK TIME: 25 MINUTES

My mom, who hates onions but loves onion dip made from the blue box, would take the packet of dried onions and crush it through a strainer until there wasn't a lick of onion string left in the dip. In her honor, I've created the exact opposite kind of dip, deeply flavored by sweet caramelized onions.

1. In a skillet, melt the bacon fat over medium-low heat. Add the onions to the hot fat and cook for 3 minutes. Use a wooden spoon to break apart any onion pieces still sticking together and continue cooking the onions, stirring every few minutes, for 20 minutes.

2. When the onions begin to get a little dry and stick to the skillet, stir in 1 teaspoon of whiskey. Alternate adding 1 teaspoon of whiskey and 1 tablespoon of water until you've used all the whiskey, then use water as needed.

3. When the onions are soft, sweet, and very brown, transfer them to a bowl and refrigerate until cold.

4. In a blender, combine the sour cream, cream cheese, salt, and garlic powder. Blend until smooth and well mixed.

5. Add the cold onions to the blender, and pulse to achieve your desired consistency. Transfer the dip to an airtight container and refrigerate for at least 1 hour. Stir the dip just before serving.

2 tablespoons bacon fat

2 onions, halved lengthwise and cut crosswise into ¼-inch-thick slices

3 teaspoons whiskey, divided

3 tablespoons water, divided

1 cup organic sour cream

½ cup organic cream cheese, at room temperature

½ teaspoon sea salt

¼ teaspoon garlic powder

PER SERVING: CALORIES: 362; TOTAL FAT: 36G;
SATURATED FAT: 19G; PROTEIN: 4G; CHOLESTEROL: 70MG;
CARBOHYDRATES: 4G; FIBER: 1G; **NET CARBS: 3G**

FAT: 87% / CARBS: 4% / PROTEIN: 9%

CREAMY DILL DEVILED EGGS

SERVES 6 / PREP TIME: 10 MINUTES / COOK TIME: 30 MINUTES

12 large free-range eggs

6 tablespoons mayonnaise

1 tablespoon dried dill

1 teaspoon sea salt

COOKING TIP *I bake the eggs Alton Brown–style. The yolks come out much creamier, and they tend to peel a lot easier, too.*

Deviled eggs are my favorite keto snack at any time of day, especially when I've made a big batch ahead of time. Dill works well with mayonnaise to create an aromatic twist on the classic deviled egg.

1. Place each whole egg in the cup of a mini-muffin tin.

2. Turn the oven to 325°F and place the muffin tin in the oven (do not preheat the oven). Bake the eggs for 30 minutes.

3. Prepare a large bowl of ice water. Transfer the eggs to the ice water and shake from side to side so they slightly crack each other. When they are cool, peel the eggs, and cut each one in half lengthwise. Scoop the yolks into a small bowl.

4. Add the mayonnaise, dill, and salt to the bowl with the yolks and mix until smooth.

5. Place the yolk mixture in a small zipper-top plastic bag. Cut off one corner of the bag at the bottom and pipe the filling into the egg halves. Serve.

PER SERVING: CALORIES: 202; TOTAL FAT: 15G; SATURATED FAT: 4G; PROTEIN: 14G; CHOLESTEROL: 376MG; CARBOHYDRATES: 3G; FIBER: 0G; **NET CARBS: 3G**

FAT: 67% / CARBS: 4% / PROTEIN: 29%

ROASTED PESTO PEPPER POPPERS

SERVES 6 / PREP TIME: 10 MINUTES / COOK TIME: 20 MINUTES

These oven-roasted pesto poppers caramelize in the oven as they bake, bringing out the natural sweetness of the peppers, balanced with a savory goat cheese and herb blend.

1. Preheat the oven to 350°F.

2. Line a rimmed baking sheet with parchment paper.

3. Lay the mini pepper halves, cut-side up, on the sheet.

4. In a small bowl, mix the pesto, goat cheese, cream cheese, shallot, and cayenne pepper sauce.

5. Fill the pepper halves with the pesto and cheese mixture. Sprinkle them with the thyme.

6. Bake for 20 minutes. Serve hot.

12 mini bell peppers, halved lengthwise and seeded

½ cup prepared pesto

¼ cup organic goat cheese

¼ cup organic cream cheese, at room temperature

2 tablespoons diced shallot

1 teaspoon cayenne pepper sauce

1 tablespoon fresh thyme leaves

PER SERVING: CALORIES: 172; TOTAL FAT: 15G;
SATURATED FAT: 5G; PROTEIN: 4G; CHOLESTEROL: 18MG;
CARBOHYDRATES: 5G; FIBER: 1G; **NET CARBS: 4G**

FAT: 79% / CARBS: 12% / PROTEIN: 9%

BUFFALO CAULIFLOWER

SERVES 4 / PREP TIME: 10 MINUTES / COOK TIME: 25 MINUTES

4 cups cauliflower florets

4 tablespoons salted grass-fed butter, at room temperature

¼ cup hot sauce

1 garlic clove, minced

¼ teaspoon paprika

¼ teaspoon sea salt

¼ teaspoon cayenne pepper

Freshly ground black pepper

Blue cheese dressing, for serving (optional)

Buffalo wings are the love of my life, but I'll take a time-out from our one-way relationship and indulge in a more snackable dish like these spicy, buttery cauliflower bites, which can be shared (unlike me with my wings).

1. Preheat the oven to 375°F.

2. Place the cauliflower florets in a large baking dish.

3. In a small microwave-safe bowl, combine the butter, hot sauce, garlic, paprika, salt, cayenne pepper, and black pepper. Microwave for 30 seconds, stir the mixture, and continue microwaving and stirring the sauce in 15-second intervals until it is smooth and creamy.

4. Pour the sauce over the cauliflower and toss to evenly coat the florets. Bake for 25 minutes.

5. Serve the cauliflower warm with a small bowl of blue cheese dressing for dipping (if using).

PER SERVING: CALORIES: 130; TOTAL FAT: 12G; SATURATED FAT: 7G; PROTEIN: 2G; CHOLESTEROL: 31MG; CARBOHYDRATES: 6G; FIBER: 3G; **NET CARBS: 3G**

FAT: 85% / CARBS: 9% / PROTEIN: 6%

ROASTED TOMATO AND GOAT CHEESE

SERVES 2 / PREP TIME: 5 MINUTES / COOK TIME: 30 MINUTES

Juicy tomatoes, sweet and spicy whiskey-caramelized onions, and refreshing goat cheese combine for this delectable dish. Enjoy on a summer evening with fresh-picked tomatoes from your garden or your local farmers' market.

1. Preheat the oven to 425°F.

2. Line a rimmed baking sheet with parchment paper.

3. Halve the tomatoes lengthwise and remove their pulp and seeds. Place the halves cut-side up on the sheet. Sprinkle the tomatoes with salt and drizzle with a bit of olive oil.

4. Add ½ tablespoon of caramelized onions to the bottom of each tomato. Add 1 tablespoon of goat cheese to each tomato. Sprinkle ¼ teaspoon of thyme on top of each tomato.

5. Bake for 30 minutes. Serve.

2 plum tomatoes

Sea salt

Extra-virgin olive oil

2 tablespoons caramelized onions, divided, from Bacon-Whiskey Caramelized Onion Dip (page 77)

4 tablespoons crumbled organic goat cheese, divided

1 teaspoon fresh thyme leaves, divided

PER SERVING: CALORIES: 101; TOTAL FAT: 8G;
SATURATED FAT: 4G; PROTEIN: 6G; CHOLESTEROL: 15MG;
CARBOHYDRATES: 4G; FIBER: 2G; **NET CARBS: 2G**

FAT: 62% / CARBS: 16% / PROTEIN: 22%

BURRATA CAPRESE SALAD

SERVES 2 TO 4 / PREP TIME: 5 MINUTES

2 medium tomatoes

Sea salt

10 fresh basil leaves

1 (8-ounce) ball organic burrata cheese

Extra-virgin olive oil

Coarsely ground black pepper

RECIPE TIP *Seasonal is always best, particularly when you're talking about sun-ripened tomatoes fresh off the vine from your garden or farmers' market. If you can't find organic burrata cheese at your local market, then make this salad with organic mozzarella cheese—it's just as delicious.*

Burrata means "buttered," and that name is spot on. Made with mozzarella and filled with sweet cream and curd, this cheese appears to melt when cut down the middle. This salad is best when eaten within 48 hours of being made.

1. Slice the tomatoes and arrange them on a plate. Sprinkle with salt.

2. Chop or tear the basil leaves and sprinkle them over the top of the tomato slices. Sprinkle with more salt.

3. Add the burrata ball to the top and drizzle it and the tomatoes with lots of olive oil. Season with salt and pepper.

4. To serve, slice the burrata and let it ooze all over the salad.

PER SERVING: CALORIES: 188; TOTAL FAT: 18G; SATURATED FAT: 4G; PROTEIN: 4G; CHOLESTEROL: 10MG; CARBOHYDRATES: 5G; FIBER: 2G; **NET CARBS: 3G**

FAT: 85% / CARBS: 6% / PROTEIN: 9%

SALAD OF BRUSSELS

SERVES 1 / PREP TIME: 5 MINUTES

If you're not a huge fan of Brussels sprouts or have never tried them, you'll be as shocked as I was that they make a ridiculously fresh and tasty salad. The adorable little leaves will make you feel like the jolly giant ghost of Christmas present, feasting on tiny little vegetables. The best part is that this salad is so simple—don't be surprised if you make it several times per week.

In a small bowl, toss together the Brussels sprouts, olive oil, lemon juice, and pepper to taste.

PER SERVING: CALORIES: 282; TOTAL FAT: 28G; SATURATED FAT: 4G; PROTEIN: 3G; CHOLESTEROL: 0MG; CARBOHYDRATES: 8G; FIBER: 3G; **NET CARBS: 5G**

FAT: 89% / CARBS: 7% / PROTEIN: 4%

1 cup chopped
Brussels sprouts

2 tablespoons
extra-virgin olive oil

1 tablespoon freshly
squeezed lemon juice

Freshly ground
black pepper

KETO TIP *Brussels sprouts are full of nutrients and fiber, but they're also a bit carby. One cup of Brussels sprouts has 4.7 net carbs, so keep your portions small.*

GARLIC PESTO GNOCCHI

SERVES 4 / PREP TIME: 30 MINUTES / COOK TIME: 10 MINUTES

1 cup fresh basil leaves

2 tablespoons pine nuts

2 garlic cloves, peeled

1 Brazil nut

Pinch ground nutmeg

¼ cup plus 2 teaspoons extra-virgin olive oil, divided

⅓ cup grated organic Parmesan cheese

4 cups shredded low-moisture organic mozzarella cheese

5 large free-range egg yolks

3 tablespoons Golden Ghee (page 224)

5 grape tomatoes

On a trip to Old Quebec City, I fell off the keto wagon for their famed maple pie. On the way home, we stopped in Stowe, Vermont. You could say I wasn't the most keto-rific spokesperson at that point, and I got the first bowl of pasta I'd eaten in eight months. I oohed and aahed through the whole meal and then spent several weekends coming up with a keto gnocchi recipe to share these savory flavors. I didn't plan to blab about my walk off the keto plank, but if anyone figures out a keto maple pie, I'll be first in line.

1. Using a mortar and pestle, coarsely grind the basil, pine nuts, garlic, Brazil nut, and nutmeg with ¼ cup of olive oil. A loose pesto is exactly what this dish calls for. Mix in the Parmesan cheese. Set aside.

2. In a medium microwave-safe bowl, microwave the mozzarella in 30-second intervals until it is melted and can be manipulated easily with your hands. Add the egg yolks to the mozzarella and hand-knead until it becomes dough-like.

3. On a piece of parchment paper, roll out the dough into two 1-foot-long rolls. Refrigerate for about 10 minutes. In the meantime, bring a large pot of salted water to a boil over high heat.

4. Using a sharp knife, cut each roll into 1-inch pieces. All at once, drop the pieces into the boiling salted water. Cook the gnocchi for 3 minutes, then drain.

5. In a large skillet, melt the ghee over medium-high heat. Add the gnocchi to the skillet and fry just until slightly crispy on both sides, about 1 minute.

6. In a separate small skillet, heat the remaining 2 teaspoons of olive oil over medium heat. Add the tomatoes. Once softened, stir in the pesto sauce just until warm, about 1 minute.

7. Pour the tomatoes and pesto over the gnocchi and toss to combine. Heat for 1 minute more and serve.

PER SERVING: CALORIES: 720; TOTAL FAT: 60G;
SATURATED FAT: 25G; PROTEIN: 42G; CHOLESTEROL: 357MG;
CARBOHYDRATES: 9G; FIBER: 2G; **NET CARBS: 7G**

FAT: 73% / CARBS: 4% / PROTEIN: 23%

BACON-RANCH BROCCOLI BITES

SERVES 4 / PREP TIME: 10 MINUTES / COOK TIME: 45 MINUTES

8 ounces uncured center-cut bacon

¾ cup organic sour cream

2 tablespoons mayonnaise

2 tablespoons Tangy Ranch Rub (page 219)

4 cups broccoli florets

1 cup shredded organic Cheddar cheese

Before keto I wasn't a broccoli eater, unless it was raw and smothered in vegetable dip. Now I can't get enough. My husband and I tried different combinations for steamed broccoli, and this salty and savory edition is a favorite.

1. Preheat the oven to 400°F.

2. Line a rimmed baking sheet with parchment paper.

3. Lay out the bacon strips evenly on the sheet. Bake the bacon to your desired crispiness, 15 to 20 minutes (no need to flip the bacon midbake). Set the bacon aside.

4. In a small bowl, mix together the sour cream, mayonnaise, and rub.

5. Put the broccoli in a large baking dish. Pour the sour cream mixture over the florets and top with the Cheddar cheese. Bake for 30 minutes.

6. Crumble the bacon over the broccoli and cheese and serve.

PER SERVING: CALORIES: 312; TOTAL FAT: 26G; SATURATED FAT: 14G; PROTEIN: 18G; CHOLESTEROL: 68MG; CARBOHYDRATES: 6G; FIBER: 2G; **NET CARBS: 4G**

FAT: 73% / CARBS: 4% / PROTEIN: 23%

PERFECT ROASTED GARLIC

SERVES 4 / PREP TIME: 10 MINUTES / COOK TIME: 1 HOUR

True to my Italian roots, there is no such thing as too much garlic. If you, too, like garlic on your garlic, serve this roasted garlic with your next steak or veggie dish. Every pillowy clove is creamy and fork-tender.

1 head elephant garlic

1 tablespoon Golden Ghee (page 224)

½ teaspoon sea salt

1 teaspoon fresh thyme leaves

1. Preheat the oven to 400°F.

2. Cut off the top (non-root end) of the garlic head, exposing most of the cloves.

3. Place the head on a sheet of aluminum foil. Add the ghee to the top of the cloves, then sprinkle with the salt and thyme. Wrap the head loosely in the foil and place it in a small baking dish in case any ghee escapes. Bake for 1 hour.

4. Use a fork to pluck out each clove. Serve as is, or blend them into a garlic paste.

PER SERVING: CALORIES: 61; TOTAL FAT: 5G; SATURATED FAT: 2G; PROTEIN: 1G; CHOLESTEROL: 0MG; CARBOHYDRATES: 3G; FIBER: 0G; **NET CARBS: 3G**

FAT: 74% / CARBS: 20% / PROTEIN: 6%

SPICY BUTTERED BEANS

SERVES 4 / PREP TIME: 5 MINUTES / COOK TIME: 10 MINUTES

4 cups trimmed
green beans

2 tablespoons Golden
Ghee (page 224)

2 garlic cloves, minced

Pinch red pepper flakes

Pinch sea salt

At about 3.5 net carbs per cup, green beans are not the keto-friendliest of all veggies. But paired with a rich blend of savory ghee and red pepper flakes, you can definitely enjoy this occasional carb "splurge."

1. Bring a medium pot of salted water to a boil. Add the green beans and cook for 3 minutes.

2. Meanwhile, prepare a bowl of ice water. Drain the green beans and immediately plunge them into the ice water to stop them from cooking. Once cooled, drain the beans and set aside.

3. In a medium skillet, melt the ghee over medium heat. When it is hot, add the garlic, red pepper flakes, and salt and cook until soft, about 1 minute.

4. Add the green beans and toss until hot, about 3 minutes. Serve.

PER SERVING: CALORIES: 93; TOTAL FAT: 8G;
SATURATED FAT: 4G; PROTEIN: 2G; CHOLESTEROL: 16MG;
CARBOHYDRATES: 8G; FIBER: 4G; **NET CARBS: 4G**

FAT: 76% / CARBS: 15% / PROTEIN: 9%

CREAMED SPINACH, ARTICHOKES, AND RED PEPPER

SERVES 8 / PREP TIME: 10 MINUTES / COOK TIME: 10 MINUTES

Imagine turning the spinach and artichoke dip you used to devour with tortilla chips into a rich and creamy side dish you can eat with a fork. The added touch of nutmeg draws out the complexity of the spinach.

1. In a medium skillet, melt the ghee over medium-high heat. When it is hot, add the spinach, artichokes, and red bell pepper. Sauté until the spinach is wilted, 5 to 10 minutes.

2. Reduce the heat to low and add the cream cheese. Stir it into the vegetables so it melts.

3. Then stir in the pesto, mayonnaise, nutmeg, and salt. Stir in the heavy cream (if using) to thin the mixture to your liking. Cook until hot, about 1 minute.

4. Transfer to a bowl and top with the Parmesan cheese. Serve.

PER SERVING: CALORIES: 237; TOTAL FAT: 23G; SATURATED FAT: 11G; PROTEIN: 4G; CHOLESTEROL: 53MG; CARBOHYDRATES: 5G; FIBER: 1G; **NET CARBS: 4G**

FAT: 85% / CARBS: 8% / PROTEIN: 7%

3 tablespoons Golden Ghee (page 224)

10 ounces baby spinach, chopped

1 (8-ounce) jar artichoke hearts, drained and chopped

½ red bell pepper, chopped

1 (8-ounce) package organic cream cheese, at room temperature, cut into pieces

2 tablespoons Roasted Garlic and Walnut Pesto (page 232) or minced garlic

¼ cup mayonnaise

½ teaspoon ground nutmeg

¼ teaspoon sea salt

2 tablespoons organic heavy (whipping) cream (optional)

¼ cup shredded organic Parmesan cheese

CAULIFLOWER RISOTTO

SERVES 4 / PREP TIME: 10 MINUTES / COOK TIME: 6 MINUTES

Florets from 1 head cauliflower

1 tablespoon minced shallot

2 tablespoons Golden Ghee (page 224)

⅓ cup organic mascarpone

1 tablespoon grated lemon zest

1 tablespoon freshly squeezed lemon juice

½ cup chopped fresh herbs, such as thyme, basil, rosemary, and/or sage

2 tablespoons shredded organic Parmesan cheese

When I was a new cook, risotto was my badge of honor. Thirty or so minutes of gently cooking rice, one tablespoon of chicken stock at a time while building my biceps with the constant stirring of a wooden spoon, and out came a creamy, velvety rice dish that was so carb-heavy it would put you into a coma after half a cup. This cauliflower version is just as delightful, minus the post-meal carb nap. Cauliflower is quickly microwaved, bathed in mascarpone and Parmesan cheese, then tossed with chopped fresh herbs.

1. Put the cauliflower florets in a food processor or blender. Pulse until the cauliflower looks like grains of rice. You will need 4 cups of riced cauliflower.

2. In a large microwave-safe bowl, combine the cauliflower, shallot, and ghee. Microwave on high for 5 minutes. Stir in the mascarpone and microwave for another minute.

3. Fold in the lemon zest, lemon juice, and herbs, and toss with the Parmesan cheese. Serve.

PER SERVING: CALORIES: 145; TOTAL FAT: 11G; SATURATED FAT: 7G; PROTEIN: 6G; CHOLESTEROL: 31MG; CARBOHYDRATES: 9G; FIBER: 4G; **NET CARBS: 5G**

FAT: 68% / CARBS: 15% / PROTEIN: 17%

CHICKEN PAD THAI

SERVES 4 / PREP TIME: 20 MINUTES / COOK TIME: 10 MINUTES

When I was a carboholic, there was a place called Jacky's Galaxie in Bristol, Rhode Island, where I got my fix for pad thai at least three times per week for lunch. It came with soup and salad (healthy, right?), and I always got a side of crab rangoon (not so healthy). I'd never loved another pad thai before and never did again, until I started keto and spent several weeks working up a keto-friendly version that includes all the peanutty and noodly goodness I craved.

1. In a medium bowl, mix the ginger, garlic powder, salt, and black pepper. Add the chicken tenders and toss until coated.

2. In a medium skillet, heat the peanut oil over medium-high heat. When the oil is hot, add the chicken tenders and cook, turning once, until cooked through, about 3 minutes. Remove the chicken from the skillet and cut into ¼-inch-thick slices. Set aside.

3. Add the eggs to the skillet and scramble them for about 1 minute. Remove the scrambled eggs from the skillet and set aside.

4. Reduce the heat under the skillet to medium-low and add the chicken broth, peanut butter, tamari, vinegar, scallion, garlic, and red pepper flakes. Stir well and cook for 3 minutes.

»

⅛ teaspoon ground ginger

⅛ teaspoon garlic powder

⅛ teaspoon sea salt

⅛ teaspoon freshly ground black pepper

2 pounds free-range chicken tenders

2 tablespoons peanut oil

3 large free-range eggs, lightly beaten

⅓ cup organic chicken broth

3 tablespoons peanut butter

2 tablespoons tamari

1 tablespoon rice vinegar

½ cup chopped scallion

2 garlic cloves, minced

1 teaspoon red pepper flakes

4 zucchini, spiralized

½ cup bean sprouts

½ cup crushed peanuts, for garnish

1 lime, cut into wedges, for garnish

KETO TIP *You can add sliced red onions and shredded carrots to your pad thai to make it more authentic, cooking them briefly after you scramble the eggs, but keep an eye on the carb count.*

5. Add the chicken slices, zucchini noodles, scrambled eggs, and sprouts to the skillet. Toss to coat with the sauce, and cook for about 1 minute.

6. Serve the pad thai garnished with the peanuts and lime wedges.

PER SERVING: CALORIES: 710; TOTAL FAT: 34G;
SATURATED FAT: 5G; PROTEIN: 90G; CHOLESTEROL: 317MG;
CARBOHYDRATES: 13G; FIBER: 5G; **NET CARBS: 8G**

FAT: 44% / CARBS: 5% / PROTEIN: 51%

CRISP BACON AND BLUE CHEESE ZOODLES

SERVES 1 / PREP TIME: 10 MINUTES

This zucchini noodle salad is packed with flavor from the crisp spinach and freshly cooked bacon, and tossed with a thick blue cheese dressing with additional blue cheese crumbles folded in.

In a large bowl, toss together the zucchini, spinach, dressing, blue cheese, bacon, and pepper to taste. Serve cold.

PER SERVING: CALORIES: 435; TOTAL FAT: 33G;
SATURATED FAT: 15G; PROTEIN: 21G; CHOLESTEROL: 75MG;
CARBOHYDRATES: 6G; FIBER: 1G; **NET CARBS: 5G**

FAT: 73% / CARBS: 6% / PROTEIN: 21%

1 cup spiralized zucchini (about 1 small zucchini), cold

½ cup baby spinach

3 tablespoons chunky blue cheese dressing

⅓ cup crumbled organic blue cheese

½ cup cooked and crumbled uncured center-cut bacon

Freshly cracked black pepper

AGLIO E OLIO ZOODLES

SERVES 1 / PREP TIME: 10 MINUTES / COOK TIME: 3 MINUTES

2 tablespoons Golden Ghee (page 224)

1 tablespoon minced garlic

Pinch red pepper flakes

2 heaping cups spiralized zucchini (about 1 medium zucchini)

Sea salt

Freshly ground black pepper

1 tablespoon grated organic Parmesan cheese

Pinch chopped fresh parsley

KETO TIP *Zucchini noodles are simple to cook, but easy to overcook. They need only 1 to 3 minutes or they'll end up soggy, making for a watery dish. Cooking them quickly and al dente will yield the best results.*

I grew up eating spaghetti aglio e olio *at least once a week. Most Italians use oil, but my grandmother used butter. I meet in the middle and use ghee in this rich, buttery, garlicky bowl of zucchini noodle goodness.* Mangiamo!

1. In a medium saucepan, melt the ghee over medium heat. Add the garlic and red pepper flakes and cook until soft but not browned, about 1 minute.

2. Add the zucchini and stir to coat the noodles. Continue cooking until hot, 1 to 2 minutes. Season with the salt and black pepper, then toss with the Parmesan cheese and parsley. Serve immediately.

PER SERVING: CALORIES: 267; TOTAL FAT: 24G; SATURATED FAT: 15G; PROTEIN: 5G; CHOLESTEROL: 64MG; CARBOHYDRATES: 9G; FIBER: 2G; **NET CARBS: 7G**

FAT: 80% / CARBS: 13% / PROTEIN: 7%

LEMON-RICOTTA ZOODLES

SERVES 2 / PREP TIME: 10 MINUTES / COOK TIME: 5 MINUTES

What I love about zucchini noodles is that they pair with just about every sauce, especially this delicate cream sauce. This dish can be served on its own or paired with chicken, fish, or pork.

1. In a small bowl, mix the ricotta cheese, zest, salt, and pepper. Set aside.

2. In a large skillet, melt the ghee over medium heat. When it is hot, add the chard and sauté until softened, 1 to 2 minutes. Add the shallot and sauté for another minute.

3. Stir in the zucchini noodles and thyme and cook until hot but still al dente, about 1 minute. Stir in the ricotta mixture and cook for another 2 minutes. Serve immediately.

PER SERVING: CALORIES: 181; TOTAL FAT: 12G; SATURATED FAT: 7G; PROTEIN: 9G; CHOLESTEROL: 36MG; CARBOHYDRATES: 8G; FIBER: 4G; **NET CARBS: 4G**

FAT: 74% / CARBS: 8% / PROTEIN: 18%

½ cup organic ricotta cheese

Grated zest of 1 lemon

Pinch sea salt

Pinch freshly ground black pepper

1 tablespoon Golden Ghee (page 224)

4 chard leaves, stemmed and chopped

½ shallot, minced

2 heaping cups spiralized zucchini (about 1 medium zucchini)

1½ teaspoons fresh thyme leaves

RECIPE TIP *Zucchini noodles became my one true veggie love after I invested in a proper vegetable spiralizer and stopped pulling muscles cranking them out with a hand zoodler.*

FRESH-CUT HERB AND BUTTER ZOODLES

SERVES 2 / PREP TIME: 10 MINUTES / COOK TIME: 4 MINUTES

¼ cup Golden Ghee
(page 224)

2 garlic cloves, minced

1 tablespoon chopped
fresh thyme leaves

1 tablespoon chopped
fresh parsley

1 tablespoon chopped
fresh basil

1 tablespoon chopped
celery leaves

2 cups spiralized
zucchini (about
1 medium zucchini)

If you have an herb garden, this is the recipe for you. Choose the leaves of your most flavorful herbs, like thyme and basil, and mix with nutrient-rich vegetable leaves like celery.

1. In a medium skillet, melt the ghee over medium heat. When it is hot, add the garlic and cook lightly until soft, about 1 minute. Stir in the thyme, parsley, basil, and celery leaves and cook for another minute.

2. Add the zucchini noodles to the pan and toss with the herbs. Cook until al dente, 1 to 2 minutes. Serve immediately.

PER SERVING: CALORIES: 265; TOTAL FAT: 26G;
SATURATED FAT: 16G; PROTEIN: 3G; CHOLESTEROL: 66MG;
CARBOHYDRATES: 9G; FIBER: 3G; **NET CARBS: 6G**

FAT: 88% / CARBS: 9% / PROTEIN: 3%

BAKED ZOODLES AND CHEESE

SERVES 6 / PREP TIME: 30 MINUTES / COOK TIME: 45 MINUTES

It's no surprise I ended up a chubby adult when the first food I cooked (and ate all of) was boxed mac and cheese. And that's how I feel about this recipe—but you can share if you want.

1. Preheat the oven to 350°F.

2. Grease a 10-inch pie dish with ghee.

3. In a large bowl, salt the zucchini to extract excess water. After 15 minutes, drain the zucchini noodles and dry them with a paper towel. Set aside on a dry paper towel to continue drying.

4. In a small bowl, whisk together the eggs, almond milk, butter, heavy cream, and garlic powder.

5. Layer the zucchini noodles in the pie dish. Cover them with the Cheddar and Monterey Jack cheeses, trying to mix them throughout the noodles. Pour the egg mixture over the noodles.

6. Bake until firm, 35 to 45 minutes. Cut into wedges and serve.

💰 💰

Golden Ghee (page 224)

1½ tablespoons sea salt

6 large, thick zucchini, spiralized

4 large free-range eggs

¾ cup unsweetened almond milk

4 tablespoons salted grass-fed butter, at room temperature

¼ cup organic heavy (whipping) cream

¼ teaspoon garlic powder

4 cups grated organic Cheddar cheese

2 cups grated organic Monterey Jack cheese

PER SERVING: CALORIES: 655; TOTAL FAT: 54G; SATURATED FAT: 33G; PROTEIN: 35G; CHOLESTEROL: 274MG; CARBOHYDRATES: 8G; FIBER: 2G; **NET CARBS: 6G**

FAT: 74% / CARBS: 5% / PROTEIN: 21%

CHAPTER SIX

FISH & SHELLFISH

GARLIC AND THYME SKILLET SALMON

SERVES 2 TO 4 / PREP TIME: 10 MINUTES / COOK TIME: 10 MINUTES

4 tablespoons Golden Ghee (page 224), divided

1 tablespoon minced garlic

1 tablespoon fresh thyme leaves

Pinch sea salt

4 (6-ounce) salmon fillets

1 shallot, quartered

¼ lemon

Salmon is a spectacularly excellent ketogenic fish because it's full of omega-3 fatty acids. Atlantic salmon has the most fat, with about 18 grams of fat per 6-ounce portion.

1. Preheat the oven to 450°F.

2. In a small bowl, mix 2 tablespoons of ghee with the garlic, thyme, and salt. Set aside.

3. In a medium cast iron skillet, melt the remaining 2 tablespoons of ghee over medium heat. When the ghee is hot, add the salmon fillets, skin-side down. Wedge the shallot quarters between each salmon fillet. Sear the fillets for 1 minute, flip, and sear for another minute.

4. Break the shallot quarters into individual layers, and top the salmon with the seasoning mixture.

5. Transfer the skillet to the oven. Bake for 8 minutes.

6. Serve the salmon and roasted shallots hot, with a squeeze of lemon.

PER SERVING: CALORIES: 684; TOTAL FAT: 47G;
SATURATED FAT: 19G; PROTEIN: 67G; CHOLESTEROL: 216MG;
CARBOHYDRATES: 2G; FIBER: 1G; **NET CARBS: 1G**

FAT: 62% / CARBS: 1% / PROTEIN: 37%

SPICY STUFFED SALMON FLORENTINE

SERVES 2 / PREP TIME: 10 MINUTES / COOK TIME: 25 MINUTES

Salmon doesn't have to be boring. In this dish, shallots and sun-dried tomatoes are enveloped in a creamy ricotta cheese mixture, sandwiched between two nutrient-packed salmon fillets.

1. Preheat the oven to 350°F.

2. Line a rimmed baking sheet with parchment paper.

3. In a small bowl, mix the cream cheese, ricotta cheese, and red pepper flakes. Set aside.

4. In a small skillet, melt the ghee over medium heat. When it is hot, add the shallot, garlic, and sun-dried tomatoes and cook until soft, 3 to 5 minutes.

5. Stir the shallot mixture into the cheese mixture.

6. Lay out 2 salmon fillets on the lined baking sheet. Spread half of the cheese mixture over the 2 fillets. Place a few spinach leaves on top of the cheese, then spread the rest of the cheese mixture on top of the spinach leaves. Rest the 2 remaining salmon fillets on top of the cheese. Season with salt and black pepper.

7. Bake until the salmon is cooked through, 15 to 20 minutes.

8. Serve with a lemon quarter on the side.

½ cup organic cream cheese, at room temperature

¼ cup organic ricotta cheese

¼ teaspoon red pepper flakes

1 tablespoon Golden Ghee (page 224)

¼ cup minced shallot

2 garlic cloves, minced

3 sun-dried tomatoes, chopped

4 thin-cut boneless, skinless salmon fillets

Fresh spinach leaves

Sea salt

Freshly ground black pepper

2 lemon quarters, for garnish

PER SERVING: CALORIES: 471; TOTAL FAT: 36G;
SATURATED FAT: 19G; PROTEIN: 32G; CHOLESTEROL: 140MG;
CARBOHYDRATES: 7G; FIBER: 1G; **NET CARBS: 6G**

FAT: 68% / CARBS: 5% / PROTEIN: 27%

BAKED HADDOCK, SAUSAGE, AND SAGE

SERVES 4 / PREP TIME: 10 MINUTES / COOK TIME: 45 MINUTES

1 pound organic
bulk sausage

2 tablespoons
chopped fresh sage

1 cup thinly sliced fennel

10 cherry tomatoes,
halved

1 onion, quartered

2 teaspoons garlic-
infused olive oil

Sea salt

Freshly ground
black pepper

2 tablespoons freshly
squeezed lemon
juice, divided

1 tablespoon grated
lemon zest

1 tablespoon
minced garlic

4 (6- to 7-ounce)
haddock fillets

Sausage and sage are a perfect marriage of savory and seasoning. When paired with haddock, they create a complex surf and turf that sends "Do you love me?" notes in class. Hint: They always check "Yes!"

1. Preheat the oven to 400°F.

2. In an ovenproof skillet, cook the sausage and sage over medium-high heat until the meat is browned and cooked through, stirring often and breaking up any large clumps, about 5 minutes. Remove the meat from the skillet, but leave any rendered fat in the skillet. Set the meat aside.

3. Add the fennel to the skillet and top it with the tomatoes and onion quarters. Drizzle the garlic olive oil over the top. Season with salt and pepper and drizzle 1 tablespoon of lemon juice over the vegetables. Place the skillet in the oven for about 30 minutes, stirring the vegetables every once in a while.

4. Meanwhile, in a medium bowl, mix the remaining 1 tablespoon of lemon juice, lemon zest, and minced garlic. Toss the haddock fillets in the mixture. Set aside.

5. When the vegetables are roasted, add the sausage to the skillet and mix well. Place the haddock fillets on top of the vegetable-sausage mix, arranging the onion quarters between each fillet so the fillets don't touch each other.

6. Bake the fillets until cooked through and flaky, about 10 minutes. Serve hot.

PER SERVING: CALORIES: 477; TOTAL FAT: 23G;
SATURATED FAT: 8G; PROTEIN: 56G; CHOLESTEROL: 177MG;
CARBOHYDRATES: 9G; FIBER: 2G; **NET CARBS: 7G**

FAT: 44% / CARBS: 8% / PROTEIN: 48%

BAKED LEMON BUTTER AND THYME COD

SERVES 2 / PREP TIME: 10 MINUTES / COOK TIME: 20 MINUTES

4 (6-ounce) cod fillets (thawed if frozen), rinsed and patted dry

Sea salt

Freshly ground black pepper

4 tablespoons salted grass-fed butter, divided

4 fresh thyme sprigs, divided

4 teaspoons freshly squeezed lemon juice, divided

COOKING TIP *It's better to leave the fish in the oven longer than to take it out too early, open the pouches, and find the fish is not cooked through. Marinating longer in the butter and lemon only adds to the flavor.*

MAKE IT PALEO *Use ghee instead of butter.*

Maybe you associate rich butter with shellfish like lobster and crab, but there's no better pair than fresh cod and butter.

1. Preheat the oven to 400°F.
2. Season the cod fillets on both sides with salt and pepper.
3. Lay out four pieces of aluminum foil, each about three times the size of a fillet. Place a fillet in the center of each piece of foil. Divide the butter, thyme, and lemon juice among the four fillets. Fold over the sides of each foil sheet to form a pouch, sealing the fillet inside. Place the four foil pouches on a rimmed baking sheet.
4. Bake for 20 minutes. Open the pouches carefully to allow the steam to escape, and serve hot.

PER SERVING: CALORIES: 284; TOTAL FAT: 18G; SATURATED FAT: 3G; PROTEIN: 32G; CHOLESTEROL: 81MG; CARBOHYDRATES: 1G; FIBER: 0G; **NET CARBS: 1G**

FAT: 55% / CARBS: 1% / PROTEIN: 44%

COFFEE-RUBBED TUNA STEAK

SERVES 2 / PREP TIME: 5 MINUTES, PLUS 30 MINUTES TO REST / COOK TIME: 5 MINUTES

Tuna steaks, appropriately named for their meaty flavor and texture, are best cooked rare. This peppery coffee rub adds a deep, smoky flavor to the tuna.

2 (4-ounce) high-quality tuna steaks

Extra-virgin olive oil

3 tablespoons finely ground coffee

1 tablespoon freshly ground black pepper

1 teaspoon sea salt

½ teaspoon ground cinnamon

½ teaspoon chili powder

1. Brush the tuna steaks with olive oil.

2. In a small bowl, combine the coffee, pepper, salt, cinnamon, and chili powder.

3. Sprinkle the coffee mixture over both sides of the tuna steaks and let them rest, bringing them to room temperature, for about 30 minutes.

4. Brush the tuna steaks with more olive oil. In a medium skillet, sear the tuna on both sides over high heat until a crust forms and the fish reaches your preferred doneness, 2 to 3 minutes per side for rare. Serve hot.

PER SERVING: CALORIES: 241; TOTAL FAT: 10G;
SATURATED FAT: 2G; PROTEIN: 34G; CHOLESTEROL: 56MG;
CARBOHYDRATES: 3G; FIBER: 1G; **NET CARBS: 2G**

FAT: 37% / CARBS: 7% / PROTEIN: 56%

BACON-WRAPPED TILAPIA

SERVES 2 TO 4 / PREP TIME: 10 MINUTES / COOK TIME: 30 MINUTES

4 (6-ounce) tilapia fillets,
rinsed and patted dry

3 tablespoons Golden
Ghee (page 224), melted

1 teaspoon dried basil

Freshly ground
black pepper

12 uncured center-cut
bacon strips

¼ cup mayonnaise

1½ tablespoons freshly
squeezed lemon juice

Anyone can wrap scallops in bacon, but why not go bigger? The smoky bacon provides a savory saltiness to this light white fish, while a delicate lemon cream sauce balances it all out.

1. Preheat the oven to 375°F.

2. Line a rimmed baking sheet with parchment paper.

3. Brush the tilapia fillets with the ghee, then sprinkle them with the basil and a few grinds of pepper. Wrap three slices of bacon around each fillet and place the wrapped fillets, bacon seams down, on the sheet.

4. Bake the fillets until cooked through and flaky, 20 to 30 minutes.

5. In a small bowl, whisk together the mayonnaise, lemon juice, and a pinch of pepper. Serve this sauce in small ramekins alongside the fish for dipping.

PER SERVING: CALORIES: 788; TOTAL FAT: 47G;
SATURATED FAT: 20G; PROTEIN: 94G; CHOLESTEROL: 272MG;
CARBOHYDRATES: 2G; FIBER: 0G; **NET CARBS: 2G**

FAT: 53% / CARBS: 1% / PROTEIN: 46%

LEMON PARMESAN–CRUSTED FISH STICKS

SERVES 2 / PREP TIME: 10 MINUTES / COOK TIME: 15 MINUTES

One of my favorite dinners as a kid was fish sticks dipped in ketchup, while watching cartoons with my cousins. My ode to those TV dinners? These crispy, flaky fish sticks that have evolved into adult-friendly dippables. I like to offer Homemade Champagne Ketchup (page 220) and/or Lemon-Dill Tartar Sauce (page 226) on the side.

1. Preheat the oven to 400°F.
2. Line a rimmed baking sheet with aluminum foil. Place a wire rack over the baking sheet and lightly grease it with a little olive oil.
3. In a small bowl, lightly beat the egg.
4. In another small bowl, combine the crushed pork rinds, Parmesan cheese, almond flour, and lemon pepper seasoning.
5. Dip each fish strip into the beaten egg, then into the dry mix, then place on the rack over the baking sheet.
6. Bake the fish sticks for 15 minutes. Serve hot with your favorite dipping sauce.

Extra-virgin olive oil

1 large free-range egg

½ cup crushed pork rinds, preferably crushed fine in a blender or food processor

¼ cup grated organic Parmesan cheese

1 tablespoon almond flour

1 teaspoon lemon pepper seasoning or Cajun seasoning

4 tilapia or cod fillets, rinsed, patted dry, and cut into 1-by-4-inch strips

PER SERVING: CALORIES: 434; TOTAL FAT: 21G; SATURATED FAT: 6G; PROTEIN: 62G; CHOLESTEROL: 222MG; CARBOHYDRATES: 4G; FIBER: 2G; **NET CARBS: 2G**

FAT: 44% / CARBS: 3% / PROTEIN: 53%

WHITE ANCHOVY AND LEMON ARUGULA SALAD

SERVES 1 / PREP TIME: 5 MINUTES / COOK TIME: 4 MINUTES

1 handful arugula

4 tablespoons extra-virgin olive oil, divided

1 tablespoon freshly squeezed lemon juice

½ teaspoon plus a pinch freshly ground black pepper

2 garlic cloves, minced

4 white anchovies

Pinch chili powder

¼ cup chopped fresh parsley

Sometimes it's the simplest ingredients that make a dish. Here, a bitter mix of arugula is complemented by fresh lemon juice and olive oil. It's full of great fats for ketogenic energy, with a modest amount of protein for a macro balance.

1. In a medium bowl, toss the arugula with 2 tablespoons of olive oil, the lemon juice, and ½ teaspoon of pepper.

2. In a small skillet, heat the remaining 2 tablespoons of olive oil over medium-high heat. Add the garlic and cook for 1 minute. Then add the anchovies and cook for about 1 minute on each side. Stir in the chili powder, parsley, and a pinch of pepper. Cook for another 30 seconds.

3. Spoon the coated anchovies on top of the arugula and serve.

PER SERVING: CALORIES: 687; TOTAL FAT: 66G; SATURATED FAT: 11G; PROTEIN: 26G; CHOLESTEROL: 60MG; CARBOHYDRATES: 5G; FIBER: 1G; **NET CARBS: 4G**

FAT: 85% / CARBS: 1% / PROTEIN: 14%

LEMON-DILL TUNA SALAD

SERVES 1 / PREP TIME: 5 MINUTES

What good is a lettuce cup if it's not filled with a scoop of tuna salad loaded with crisp, fresh ingredients like celery, onion, and dill? For an extra kick, add a tablespoon of dill pickle relish.

In a small bowl, combine the tuna, celery, onion, dill, mayonnaise, and lemon pepper seasoning. Use a fork to mix well.

PER SERVING: CALORIES: 230; TOTAL FAT: 8G;
SATURATED FAT: 2G; PROTEIN: 36G; CHOLESTEROL: 81MG;
CARBOHYDRATES: 3G; FIBER: 1G; **NET CARBS: 2G**

FAT: 32% / CARBS: 4% / PROTEIN: 64%

1 (6-ounce) can water-packed chunk white tuna

1 tablespoon chopped celery

1 tablespoon chopped white onion

1 tablespoon chopped fresh dill

1 tablespoon mayonnaise

1 teaspoon lemon pepper seasoning

CREAMY SEAFOOD CHOWDER

SERVES 6 / PREP TIME: 10 MINUTES / COOK TIME: 1 HOUR

3 tablespoons Golden Ghee (page 224)

1 ounce salt pork

½ white onion, diced

1 teaspoon minced garlic

1½ cups clam juice

1 cup Lemon-Rosemary Bone Broth (page 193) or organic chicken broth

½ teaspoon celery salt

½ teaspoon dried tarragon

¼ teaspoon dried thyme

1 bay leaf

1 pound minced clams

1 pound frozen precooked langostinos, defrosted overnight in the refrigerator

1 cup organic heavy (whipping) cream

3 dashes Worcestershire sauce

½ teaspoon sea salt

1 teaspoon freshly ground black pepper

MAKE IT PALEO *Make this recipe Rhode Island–style by omitting the heavy cream. The flavor will be light and delightfully brothy.*

Growing up in the Northeast I've had the pleasure of sampling three different styles of clam chowder: Rhode Island (clear broth), New England (creamy broth), and Manhattan (red broth). But for me, there's nothing like a creamy, peppery clam chowder. Most clam chowders are full of carbs, so instead of potatoes, I've added more protein with langostinos, which look and taste like tiny lobsters. If you're on a budget, you can certainly skip them and just call it clam chowder. And as all New Englanders know, clam chowder is not just for the winter—it's year-round deliciousness.

1. In a medium saucepan, melt the ghee over medium heat. When it is hot, add the salt pork, onion, and garlic and cook until the onion softens, about 5 minutes.

2. Add the clam juice, broth, celery salt, tarragon, thyme, and bay leaf. Bring the liquid to a simmer, reduce the heat to medium-low, and simmer for 30 minutes.

3. Add the clams and langostinos to the pot. Increase the heat and bring the liquid to a boil, then reduce the heat to low and simmer the soup until the clams and langostinos are hot, 5 to 10 minutes.

4. Stir in the heavy cream, Worcestershire sauce, salt, and pepper. Simmer for another 10 minutes.

5. Remove the salt pork and serve.

PER SERVING: CALORIES: 348; TOTAL FAT: 26G; SATURATED FAT: 16G; PROTEIN: 25G; CHOLESTEROL: 106MG; CARBOHYDRATES: 4G; FIBER: 0G; **NET CARBS: 4G**

FAT: 67% / CARBS: 5% / PROTEIN: 28%

CAJUN CRAB AND SPAGHETTI SQUASH

SERVES 4 / PREP TIME: 10 MINUTES / COOK TIME: 45 MINUTES

When I visited the French Quarter of New Orleans, I left with completely new taste buds that craved Cajun dishes nonstop. In this recipe the naturally sweet spaghetti squash combines with the Cajun spices and cream sauce to make for a sweet and savory combo that's totally addicting. It has mesmerized many of my non-keto guests. It's one of my all-time favorite recipes and I'm excited to share it with you.

1. Use a fork to poke holes all over the spaghetti squash. Microwave the squash on high for about 15 minutes and then let it cool for 10 minutes. Cut the squash in half and remove the seeds. Scoop the squash "noodles" into a large bowl and set aside.

2. In a medium skillet, melt the ghee over medium heat. Stir in 2 tablespoons of Cajun seasoning. Add the crabmeat and toss it in the ghee to coat it. Transfer the crab to a small bowl and set aside.

3. Add the heavy cream, butter, garlic salt, cayenne pepper, black pepper, and remaining 1 teaspoon of Cajun seasoning to the skillet and bring it to a simmer, then reduce the heat to low. Stir in the spaghetti squash and cook until the liquid reduces by half and sticks to the squash, about 20 minutes (the sauce will thicken more upon cooling, too).

4. Toss in the crab and heat until hot, about 1 minute, and then remove the skillet from the heat. Serve immediately.

1 medium spaghetti squash

3 tablespoons Golden Ghee (page 224)

2 tablespoons plus 1 teaspoon Cajun seasoning, divided

Meat from 1 pound cooked Alaskan king crab legs

2 cups organic heavy (whipping) cream

3 tablespoons salted grass-fed butter

1 teaspoon garlic salt

½ teaspoon cayenne pepper

⅛ teaspoon freshly ground black pepper

RECIPE TIP *If you're not feeling crabby, grill some chicken instead. It's just as good.*

PER SERVING: CALORIES: 724; TOTAL FAT: 69G; SATURATED FAT: 43G; PROTEIN: 22G; CHOLESTEROL: 265MG; CARBOHYDRATES: 10G; FIBER: 2G; **NET CARBS: 8G**

FAT: 83% / CARBS: 5% / PROTEIN: 12%

CAJUN SNOW CRAB BOIL

SERVES 2 / PREP TIME: 5 MINUTES / COOK TIME: 10 MINUTES

1 lemon, quartered

3 tablespoons
Cajun seasoning

2 bay leaves

4 frozen precooked
snow crab legs,
defrosted overnight
in the refrigerator

Golden Ghee (page 224),
melted, for serving

If you've spent any time in Louisiana, I'm sure Cajun flavors are a priority for your palate. This simple Cajun crab boil tastes straight out of the bayou. I call for snow crabs, but fresh blue crabs work great, too. Throw on your beads and enjoy.

1. Fill a large pot halfway with salted water and bring it to a boil over high heat. Squeeze the juice from the lemon quarters into the pot and then toss in the quarters. Add the Cajun seasoning and bay leaves and let the seasoned water boil for 1 minute.

2. Add the crab legs to the pot, making sure they're completely covered in water. Boil them for 5 to 8 minutes, making sure they stay submerged the whole time.

3. Serve with a small ramekin of melted ghee for dipping.

PER SERVING: CALORIES: 643; TOTAL FAT: 51G;
SATURATED FAT: 32G; PROTEIN: 41G; CHOLESTEROL: 232MG;
CARBOHYDRATES: 4G; FIBER: 1G; **NET CARBS: 3G**

FAT: 71% / CARBS: 4% / PROTEIN: 25%

CREAMY LANGOSTINOS NORMANDY

SERVES 4 / PREP TIME: 10 MINUTES / COOK TIME: 40 MINUTES

It took more than 30 years for me to try lobster and another two before I liked it. It took a trip to Maine for my taste buds to turn, and then I spent a week in Boothbay Harbor eating sweet, buttery Maine lobster for as many meals as I could get it. I haven't looked back. This creamy dish uses sweet, tender, and affordable lobster-like langostinos. (If your pockets are padded, you can use lobster instead.) This is a beloved regular at our family holiday parties.

1. Drain any excess water from the langostinos and pat dry with a paper towel.

2. In a large skillet, melt the ghee over medium heat. When it is hot, add the langostinos and cook until hot, about 5 minutes. Transfer the langostinos to a small bowl using a slotted spoon and set aside.

3. Add the shallot to the skillet and cook until soft, about 3 minutes. Stir in the heavy cream, ketchup, Worcestershire sauce, and salt. Bring the sauce to a simmer, stirring frequently, then reduce the heat to low and simmer until it reduces to your preferred consistency, 20 to 30 minutes. Add the sherry and stir for another minute.

4. Stir the langostinos into the sauce until heated through, about 1 minute, and serve hot.

PER SERVING: CALORIES: 241; TOTAL FAT: 21G; SATURATED FAT: 13G; PROTEIN: 9G; CHOLESTEROL: 116MG; CARBOHYDRATES: 4G; FIBER: 0G; **NET CARBS: 4G**

FAT: 78% / CARBS: 7% / PROTEIN: 15%

2 cups frozen precooked langostinos, defrosted overnight in the refrigerator

3 tablespoons Golden Ghee (page 224)

1 shallot, minced

1 cup organic heavy (whipping) cream

¼ cup Homemade Champagne Ketchup (page 220)

1 tablespoon Worcestershire sauce

1 teaspoon sea salt

4 teaspoons dry sherry

RECIPE TIP *Langostinos are not only less expensive than lobster but also sweeter and more tender. You can find them in the freezer section of most grocery stores, but I prefer those at my local fish market; some frozen precooked brands are overcooked.*

LEMON CREAM ZOODLES WITH SWEET MAINE LOBSTER

SERVES 2 / PREP TIME: 10 MINUTES / COOK TIME: 10 MINUTES

½ cup organic
chicken broth

1½ cups organic heavy
(whipping) cream

1 teaspoon minced garlic

1 lemon, quartered
and seeded

2 zucchini, spiralized

¼ cup Golden Ghee
(page 224)

2 cups frozen precooked
Maine lobster meat,
defrosted overnight
in the refrigerator

RECIPE TIP *When overcooked, zucchini makes a
dish soupy. To avoid this,
salt your spiralized zucchini
before cooking to draw out
excess moisture. Then use
paper towels to dry the
zucchini noodles—the drier,
the better.*

*Lobster makes any occasion a special one. Juicy
Maine lobster should be your first choice, but if you
need to be more practical, shrimp work deliciously
in this recipe, as well.*

1. In a medium skillet, bring the chicken broth to a
   boil over medium heat. Reduce the heat to low and
   stir in the heavy cream, garlic, and lemon quarters. Simmer, stirring frequently, until the liquid
   is reduced by half, 5 to 10 minutes. Discard the
   lemon quarters.

2. Stir the zucchini noodles into the cream sauce and
   cook until al dente, about 2 minutes.

3. Meanwhile, in a small saucepan, melt the ghee
   over medium heat. When it is hot, add the lobster
   and heat until hot, about 1 minute.

4. Stir the lobster and ghee into the zucchini and
   cream sauce and serve immediately.

PER SERVING: CALORIES: 1,037; TOTAL FAT: 92G;
SATURATED FAT: 61G; PROTEIN: 30G; CHOLESTEROL: 452MG;
CARBOHYDRATES: 7G; FIBER: 2G; **NET CARBS: 5G**

FAT: 85% / CARBS: 3% / PROTEIN: 12%

SPICY LOBSTER SALAD

SERVES 1 / PREP TIME: 10 MINUTES

I've joined the ranks of the New England cold lobster crew, and lobster salad has an anchor on my heart. This creamy, spicy version is my go-to. Enjoy it in fresh lettuce cups or on Baked Parmesan Chips (page 69).

1. In a medium bowl, mix the mayonnaise, lemon juice, sriracha, tarragon, and salt.
2. Stir in the lobster and celery until well mixed. Serve.

⅓ cup mayonnaise

1 tablespoon freshly squeezed lemon juice

1 teaspoon sriracha

1½ teaspoons minced fresh tarragon

Pinch sea salt

1 cup frozen precooked Maine lobster meat, defrosted overnight in the refrigerator

¼ cup chopped celery

PER SERVING: CALORIES: 91; TOTAL FAT: 9G; SATURATED FAT: 1G; PROTEIN: 2G; CHOLESTEROL: 6MG; CARBOHYDRATES: 2G; FIBER: 0G; **NET CARBS: 2G**

FAT: 85% / CARBS: 7% / PROTEIN: 8%

BACON UNWRAPPED SCALLOPS

SERVES 3 TO 4 / PREP TIME: 10 MINUTES / COOK TIME: 30 MINUTES

1 pound uncured center-cut bacon

2 pounds fresh sea scallops, patted dry

¼ cup dry white wine

3 tablespoons Golden Ghee (page 224)

Lemon wedges

Bacon-wrapped scallops are so popular as pass-arounds at parties that they can be found in the frozen food aisle. These take a little more time than the boxed version, but I think you'll agree they taste much better.

1. Preheat the oven to 400°F.

2. Line two rimmed baking sheets with parchment paper.

3. Lay out the bacon strips evenly on the sheets. Bake until crispy, 15 to 20 minutes (no need to flip the bacon midbake). Once the bacon has cooled, crumble it into a small bowl.

4. Pour the bacon grease from the baking sheets into a medium skillet and set it over high heat.

5. Brown the scallops in the hot grease, 3 to 4 minutes per side. Remove the scallops and set aside.

6. Add the wine to the skillet and deglaze the pan by scraping up any browned bits from the bottom (this is where the real flavor comes from). Stir the ghee into the wine to make a sauce.

7. Add the crumbled bacon and scallops to the skillet and toss to coat with the sauce and heat through, 1 minute. Divide the scallops and sauce between plates and squeeze lemon over the top. Serve.

PER SERVING: CALORIES: 550; TOTAL FAT: 27G; SATURATED FAT: 13G; PROTEIN: 66G; CHOLESTEROL: 179MG; CARBOHYDRATES: 7G; FIBER: 0G; **NET CARBS: 7G**

FAT: 44% / CARBS: 8% / PROTEIN: 48%

SAFFRON TOMATO SHRIMP

SERVES 2 / PREP TIME: 10 MINUTES / COOK TIME: 25 MINUTES

Shrimp is such a simple dish to put together; all you need to find is the right flavor combinations. This dish is infused with the flavors of saffron and the spice of a scampi. Serve as is or over hot zucchini noodles.

2 tablespoons Golden Ghee (page 224)

½ fennel bulb, cored and chopped

20 medium cooked shrimp

2 garlic cloves, minced

Pinch saffron

Pinch smoked paprika

1 tomato, chopped

½ cup organic chicken broth

1 tablespoon freshly squeezed lemon juice

Pinch white pepper

Pinch cayenne pepper

1. In a medium skillet, melt the ghee over medium heat. When it is hot, add the fennel and sauté until soft, about 3 minutes. Stir in the shrimp, garlic, saffron, and paprika. Continue cooking until the shrimp is heated through, about 1 minute. If the skillet becomes too dry, add a little more ghee.

2. Stir in the tomato, broth, lemon juice, white pepper, and cayenne pepper. Bring the liquid to a simmer and reduce by half, about 20 minutes. Serve immediately.

PER SERVING: CALORIES: 333; TOTAL FAT: 13G; SATURATED FAT: 8G; PROTEIN: 45G; CHOLESTEROL: 353MG; CARBOHYDRATES: 11G; FIBER: 2G; **NET CARBS: 9G**

FAT: 35% / CARBS: 11% / PROTEIN: 54%

SATURDAY GARLIC SHRIMP

SERVES 2 / PREP TIME: 10 MINUTES / COOK TIME: 10 MINUTES

2 tablespoons Golden Ghee (page 224)

2 garlic cloves, minced

20 medium shrimp, peeled and deveined

Pinch red pepper flakes

Pinch sea salt

Pinch freshly ground black pepper

1 tablespoon organic Parmesan cheese

MAKE IT PALEO *Simply nix the Parmesan cheese.*

This is a very simple recipe, perfect after a long week. Bonus—it fills the house with a heavenly garlic scent. You can serve the shrimp on its own, or toss in two heaping cups of zucchini noodles for about one minute.

1. In a large skillet, melt the ghee over medium-high heat. When it is hot, add the garlic and cook for 1 to 2 minutes. The garlic should not brown. Add the shrimp and cook for about 2 minutes. Stir in the red pepper flakes, salt, and pepper. Sauté the shrimp until they are cooked through, about 5 minutes more.

2. Stir in the Parmesan cheese and serve.

PER SERVING: CALORIES: 308; TOTAL FAT: 14G; SATURATED FAT: 8G; PROTEIN: 43G; CHOLESTEROL: 355MG; CARBOHYDRATES: 4G; FIBER: 0G; **NET CARBS: 4G**

FAT: 41% / CARBS: 4% / PROTEIN: 55%

SHRIMP TACOS WITH AVOCADO

SERVES 2 / PREP TIME: 10 MINUTES, PLUS 30 MINUTES TO MARINATE / COOK TIME: 10 MINUTES

These tacos are made with a delicious blend of cheeses and shrimp marinated in a spicy blend of jalapeños, lime juice, and cilantro.

TO MAKE THE SHRIMP

In a single-serving blender or mini food processor, blend the olive oil, lime juice, cilantro, garlic, jalapeño, red pepper flakes, salt, and black pepper. Pour the mixture into a zipper-top plastic bag or sealable container. Add the shrimp, toss to coat the shrimp in the marinade, and refrigerate for at least 30 minutes.

TO MAKE THE TACO SHELLS

1. Preheat the oven to 350°F.

2. Line a rimmed baking sheet with parchment paper.

3. In a medium bowl, combine the Cheddar, Monterey Jack, and Colby cheeses. Form six 4-inch cheese circles on the sheet. Bake until browned around the edges, about 5 minutes.

4. Using a spatula, flip one side of each circle onto the other side to form the taco "shells." Do this very quickly, before the cheese has a chance to cool.

5. In a medium skillet, sauté the marinated shrimp over medium-high heat until cooked through, about 5 minutes.

»

FOR THE SHRIMP

2 tablespoons extra-virgin olive oil

1 teaspoon freshly squeezed lime juice

½ cup chopped fresh cilantro

1 garlic clove

½ jalapeño pepper, halved and seeded

¼ teaspoon red pepper flakes

1 teaspoon sea salt

1 teaspoon freshly ground black pepper

10 medium shrimp, peeled and deveined

FOR THE TACO SHELLS

1 cup shredded organic Cheddar cheese

½ cup shredded organic Monterey Jack cheese

½ cup shredded organic Colby cheese

FOR SERVING

1 teaspoon grated
lime zest

1 avocado, peeled,
pitted, and chopped

1 tablespoon minced
red onion

RECIPE TIP *Using a 2-cup
bag of shredded organic Mexican blend cheese is a cheap
and simple way to make
this recipe.*

MAKE IT PALEO *Who
says you even need a taco
shell? This shrimp recipe is
just as delicious skewered
and grilled!*

TO ASSEMBLE AND SERVE

Divide the shrimp between the taco "shells" and
top with the lime zest, avocado, and red onion.
Serve immediately.

———

PER SERVING: CALORIES: 958; TOTAL FAT: 80G;
SATURATED FAT: 30G; PROTEIN: 54G; CHOLESTEROL: 348MG;
CARBOHYDRATES: 12G; FIBER: 8G; **NET CARBS: 4G**

FAT: 73% / CARBS: 5% / PROTEIN: 22%

SPICY SRIRACHA SHRIMP

SERVES 2 / PREP TIME: 10 MINUTES / COOK TIME: 10 MINUTES

These shrimp make a nice snack, but if you toss in zucchini noodles for the last minute of cooking, you'll have a delicious, complete meal.

1. In a small bowl, mix the garlic, turmeric, salt, pepper, and saffron.

2. In a large skillet, melt the ghee over medium heat. Add the onion and cook until softened, 3 to 5 minutes. Stir in the spice mixture and cook for 2 minutes. Stir in the sriracha.

3. Add the shrimp and sauté until cooked through, about 5 minutes. Serve immediately.

PER SERVING: CALORIES: 395; TOTAL FAT: 19G;
SATURATED FAT: 11G; PROTEIN: 48G; CHOLESTEROL: 487MG;
CARBOHYDRATES: 5G; FIBER: 0G; **NET CARBS: 5G**

FAT: 45% / CARBS: 5% / PROTEIN: 50%

1 tablespoon minced garlic

1 teaspoon ground turmeric

Pinch sea salt

Pinch freshly ground black pepper

Pinch saffron

3 tablespoons Golden Ghee (page 224)

½ onion, chopped

2 tablespoons sriracha

1 pound medium shrimp, peeled and deveined

CHAPTER SEVEN
BEEF & LAMB

GARLIC-THYME BEEF FONDUE

SERVES 4 TO 6 / PREP TIME: 10 MINUTES / COOK TIME: 10 MINUTES

4 cups organic beef broth

1 cup dry red wine

1 shallot, chopped

2 tablespoons
minced garlic

1 tablespoon sea salt

1 tablespoon freshly
ground black pepper

3 fresh thyme sprigs

Thin slices of grass-fed
beef filet and/or
free-range chicken

KETO TIP *Keep in mind that
all the carbs in this dish are
in the broth you use to cook.*

*Fondue is one of my favorite dinners because it can
be shared with just a few or many. Most people think
fondue is limited to cheese or chocolate, but you can
make delicious broths and oils to cook meat in, too.*

1. In an electric fondue pot set on high, combine the
   beef broth, red wine, shallot, garlic, salt, pepper,
   and thyme. Heat to a simmer.

2. Use fondue forks to cook single pieces of meat at
   a time. Each piece will take 1 to 3 minutes to reach
   your preferred doneness.

PER SERVING (½ POUND MEAT): CALORIES: 169; TOTAL FAT: 9G;
SATURATED FAT: 3G; PROTEIN: 18G; CHOLESTEROL: 48MG;
CARBOHYDRATES: 5G; FIBER: 1G; **NET CARBS: 4G**

FAT: 48% / CARBS: 9% / PROTEIN: 43%

VEGGIE FRIED BEEF

SERVES 4 / PREP TIME: 10 MINUTES / COOK TIME: 10 MINUTES

Forget all those bowls of fried rice you ate from your local Chinese place: they're dead to you. But you won't be upset about laying flowers on the grave of your old bowl of soy-soaked rice when you try this recipe. Imagine that crumbled beef takes the main stage here, and when combined with fresh veggies, you'll get a savory dish with the crunch of fresh pea pods and broccoli.

1. In a medium skillet, brown the ground beef over medium-high heat, about 3 minutes. Remove the beef from the pan, but leave some rendered grease in the skillet.

2. Reduce the heat to medium and crack the eggs into the skillet, stirring to scramble them, about 1 minute.

3. Return the meat to the skillet. Stir in the tamari, peanut butter, ginger, pea pods, broccoli, and scallion. Cover and cook for 5 minutes, then stir and serve.

1 pound grass-fed ground beef

3 large free-range eggs

1 tablespoon tamari

1 tablespoon peanut butter

⅛ teaspoon ground ginger

1 cup pea pods, trimmed

¼ cup chopped broccoli

1 scallion, chopped

PER SERVING: CALORIES: 297; TOTAL FAT: 13G; SATURATED FAT: 4G; PROTEIN: 42G; CHOLESTEROL: 224MG; CARBOHYDRATES: 5G; FIBER: 2G; **NET CARBS: 3G**

FAT: 39% / CARBS: 6% / PROTEIN: 55%

BACON AND ONION–WRAPPED MEATBALLS

SERVES 6 / PREP TIME: 20 MINUTES / COOK TIME: 30 MINUTES

1 pound grass-fed ground beef

1 pound free-range ground pork

2 large free-range eggs, lightly beaten

1 cup grated organic Parmesan cheese

1 cup shredded organic mozzarella cheese

¾ cup minced garlic or garlic paste

2 teaspoons freshly ground black pepper

1 tablespoon Italian seasoning

2 or 3 onions (only the outer layers are used)

1 pound uncured center-cut bacon

Would a meatball by any other name smell as good? Yes, actually, when it's wrapped in savory roasted onion that's fiercely hugged by salty bacon.

1. Preheat the oven to 350°F.

2. Line a rimmed baking sheet with parchment paper.

3. In a large bowl, combine the beef, pork, eggs, Parmesan and mozzarella cheeses, garlic, pepper, and Italian seasoning. Use your hands to mix the ingredients well and form them into meatballs that are large enough to fill the onion shells in step 4.

4. Cut the top and bottom off each onion and then separate the layers. Stuff each onion shell with a meatball. Wrap each onion ball with bacon. Place each wrapped meatball on the baking sheet.

5. Bake until the meatballs are cooked through, about 30 minutes. Serve hot.

PER SERVING: CALORIES: 510; TOTAL FAT: 23G; SATURATED FAT: 10G; PROTEIN: 65G; CHOLESTEROL: 226MG; CARBOHYDRATES: 10G; FIBER: 1G; **NET CARBS: 9G**

FAT: 42% / CARBS: 7% / PROTEIN: 51%

CHEESE BOMB ITALIAN MEATBALLS

SERVES 5 / PREP TIME: 20 MINUTES / COOK TIME: 20 MINUTES

No Italian grandmas are required for this recipe, and don't even think of adding soggy bread crumbs. Serve these tender, cheesy meatballs with Rhode Island Red Marinara Sauce (page 221) over hot zucchini noodles instead of pasta.

1. Preheat the oven to 400°F.

2. Line a rimmed baking sheet with parchment paper.

3. In a large bowl, combine the beef, pork, egg, water, mozzarella and Parmesan cheeses, garlic, Italian seasoning, Cajun seasoning, salt, and pepper. Use your hands to mix thoroughly. Form the mixture into meatballs of your preferred size (keep in mind that they will shrink when they cook).

4. Cut the fresh mozzarella into cubes, one for each meatball. Stuff a cube into each meatball, making sure to reseal the meatballs smoothly all the way around. Place each stuffed meatball on the baking sheet.

5. Bake the meatballs until they are cooked through, about 20 minutes. Serve hot.

PER SERVING: CALORIES: 521; TOTAL FAT: 23G;
SATURATED FAT: 11G; PROTEIN: 72G; CHOLESTEROL: 220MG;
CARBOHYDRATES: 4G; FIBER: 0G; **NET CARBS: 4G**

FAT: 40% / CARBS: 5% / PROTEIN: 55%

1 pound grass-fed ground beef

1 pound free-range ground pork

1 large free-range egg, lightly beaten

1 tablespoon water

½ cup shredded organic mozzarella cheese

½ cup freshly grated organic Parmesan cheese

1 tablespoon minced garlic

1 tablespoon Italian seasoning

1 teaspoon Cajun seasoning

1 teaspoon sea salt

1 teaspoon freshly ground black pepper

1 (8-ounce) ball fresh organic mozzarella cheese

RECIPE TIP *The finished meatballs freeze well, so make a large batch and then save them for work lunches and quick dinners.*

MEATZZA

SERVES 2 TO 3 / PREP TIME: 10 MINUTES / COOK TIME: 30 MINUTES

Grass-fed butter, at room temperature

8 ounces grass-fed ground beef

8 ounces free-range ground pork

½ cup grated organic Parmesan cheese

2 tablespoons water

1½ teaspoons pizza seasoning

1 teaspoon fennel seed

½ cup Rhode Island Red Marinara Sauce (page 221)

1 cup shredded organic mozzarella cheese

¼ cup chopped green bell pepper

¼ cup chopped red onion

The concept of meat on pizza isn't new. Ground beef, ground sausage, even shaved steak works. In this ketogenic version, the pizza is flipped upside down, so the meat is the "crust," and then topped with cheese, sauce, and some fresh fixins.

1. Preheat the oven to 400°F.

2. Butter a 9-inch pie dish.

3. In a large bowl, mix the beef, pork, Parmesan cheese, water, pizza seasoning, and fennel. Flatten out this mixture in the bottom of the pie dish.

4. Bake until the meat has browned, 15 to 20 minutes. (If desired, blot any excess oil with paper towels.)

5. Top the meat crust with the marinara, mozzarella cheese, green bell pepper, and onion. Bake for another 10 minutes. Slice and serve.

PER SERVING: CALORIES: 659; TOTAL FAT: 31G; SATURATED FAT: 16G; PROTEIN: 91G; CHOLESTEROL: 241MG; CARBOHYDRATES: 7G; FIBER: 3G; **NET CARBS: 4G**

FAT: 42% / CARBS: 3% / PROTEIN: 55%

PHILLY CHEESESTEAK MEATLOAF

SERVES 4 / PREP TIME: 10 MINUTES / COOK TIME: 45 MINUTES

If you love a good Philly cheesesteak, then you'll love this cheesy meatloaf filled with sweet onion and pepper, which is easy to make—and even easier to devour.

1. Preheat the oven to 350°F.

2. In a large bowl, mix the beef, onion, green bell pepper, heavy cream, Worcestershire sauce, salt, pepper, garlic powder, and onion powder.

3. Spread half of the meatloaf mixture in the bottom of a baking dish. Top it with 2 cups of American cheese. Layer the remaining meatloaf on top of the cheese and top it with the remaining 2 cups of American cheese.

4. Bake for 45 minutes. Let sit for 5 minutes, then slice and serve.

PER SERVING: CALORIES: 656; TOTAL FAT: 44G; SATURATED FAT: 25G; PROTEIN: 56G; CHOLESTEROL: 223MG; CARBOHYDRATES: 10G; FIBER: 1G; **NET CARBS: 9G**

FAT: 60% / CARBS: 5% / PROTEIN: 35%

1 pound grass-fed ground beef

½ yellow onion, chopped

1 green bell pepper, seeded and chopped

⅓ cup organic heavy (whipping) cream

2 tablespoons Worcestershire sauce

1 teaspoon sea salt

½ teaspoon freshly ground black pepper

½ teaspoon garlic powder

½ teaspoon onion powder

4 cups shredded organic American cheese, divided

FIVE-LAYER MEXICAN CASSEROLE

SERVES 6 / PREP TIME: 10 MINUTES / COOK TIME: 20 MINUTES

2 ripe avocados, peeled, pitted, and cut into chunks

1 tablespoon freshly squeezed lime juice

¼ cup chopped fresh cilantro

¼ cup diced white onion

1 tomato, seeded and chopped

1 teaspoon minced garlic

½ teaspoon sea salt

2 pounds grass-fed ground beef

¼ cup water

¼ cup Golden Taco Seasoning (page 217)

2 cups organic sour cream

2 cups shredded lettuce

2 cups shredded organic Cheddar cheese

Cayenne pepper sauce

Who says Mexican layer dip is only for Super Bowl parties and cookouts, when you can add enough meat to make a spicy base that eats like a casserole? This dish comes to the table with a hefty handshake of spicy taco beef, and then it's topped with cool sour cream and hearty guacamole, followed by fresh lettuce and sharp Cheddar cheese. Spicy cayenne pepper sauce is the final high-five on this dish.

1. In a medium bowl, mash together the avocado, lime juice, cilantro, onion, tomato, garlic, and salt. Cover the guacamole with plastic wrap and refrigerate while you make the rest of the casserole.

2. In a medium skillet, cook the ground beef over medium heat until it is browned and crumbled, about 10 minutes. Stir in the water and taco seasoning. Reduce the heat to simmer and cook for 10 minutes.

3. Transfer the meat to the bottom of a 9-by-9-inch dish. Top it with the sour cream. Top the sour cream with the guacamole. Scatter the lettuce over the guacamole and top it with the Cheddar cheese. Drizzle on some cayenne pepper sauce and serve.

PER SERVING: CALORIES: 720; TOTAL FAT: 52G; SATURATED FAT: 24G; PROTEIN: 60G; CHOLESTEROL: 208MG; CARBOHYDRATES: 10G; FIBER: 7G; **NET CARBS: 3G**

FAT: 66% / CARBS: 2% / PROTEIN: 32%

SWEDISH MEATBALLS

SERVES 4 / PREP TIME: 10 MINUTES / COOK TIME: 2½ HOURS

My get-togethers wouldn't be the same without a crockpot of Swedish meatballs. These babies are baked in the oven, and then simmered in a slow cooker for a few hours until they're soft and rich. Serve over lightly sautéed zucchini noodles.

1. Preheat the oven to 400°F.

2. Line a large baking pan with parchment paper.

3. In a large bowl, combine the beef, pork, Cheddar cheese, egg, water, onion, nutmeg, and allspice. Roll the mixture into 1½-inch meatballs and put them in the lined baking pan.

4. Bake for 20 minutes.

5. Meanwhile, in a small skillet, heat the butter, chicken broth, and heavy cream over medium heat. Once it begins to simmer, reduce the heat to low and let it simmer until it reduces by half, about 20 minutes. Then, stir in the mustard and Worcestershire sauce.

6. Pour the sauce into the slow cooker, and add the meatballs when they're ready. Cook on low for 2 hours. Serve.

1 pound grass-fed ground beef

1 pound free-range ground pork

1 cup shredded mild organic Cheddar cheese

1 large free-range egg

1 tablespoon water

¼ cup diced onion

¼ teaspoon ground nutmeg

¼ teaspoon ground allspice

4 tablespoons salted grass-fed butter

1½ cups organic chicken broth

1½ cups organic heavy (whipping) cream

1 tablespoon Dijon mustard

1 tablespoon Worcestershire sauce

PER SERVING: CALORIES: 773; TOTAL FAT: 50G; SATURATED FAT: 28G; PROTEIN: 74G; CHOLESTEROL: 347MG; CARBOHYDRATES: 3G; FIBER: 0G; **NET CARBS: 3G**

FAT: 58% / CARBS: 3% / PROTEIN: 39%

MEATBALL PARMESAN SPAGHETTI SQUASH

SERVES 5 / PREP TIME: 20 MINUTES / COOK TIME: 45 MINUTES

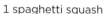

1 spaghetti squash

2 cups Rhode Island
Red Marinara Sauce
(page 221)

1 pound grass-fed
ground beef

1 cup grated organic
Parmesan cheese

1 large free-range egg

1 teaspoon minced garlic

1 teaspoon chili powder

1 teaspoon sea salt

½ teaspoon freshly
ground black pepper

½ teaspoon dried oregano

½ teaspoon dried basil

1 tablespoon extra-virgin
olive oil

2 to 4 cups shredded
organic mozzarella cheese

Spaghetti squash "noodles" are heavier than zoo-dles, but they add a natural sweetness to sauces. The savory tomato sauce and meatballs, mixed with zesty Parmesan and gooey mozzarella, pair naturally with the slightly sweet spaghetti squash.

1. Preheat the oven to 350°F.

2. Line a rimmed baking sheet with parchment paper.

3. Use a fork to poke holes all over the spaghetti squash. Microwave the squash on high for about 15 minutes and then let it cool for 10 minutes. Cut the squash in half and remove the seeds. Scoop the squash "noodles" into a large bowl and set aside. Reserve the spaghetti squash shell halves.

4. Meanwhile, in a medium saucepan, heat the marinara sauce over medium heat until hot, then lower the heat to a simmer.

5. In a large bowl, combine the ground beef, Parmesan cheese, egg, garlic, chili powder, salt, pepper, oregano, and basil. Use your hands to mix the ingredients well and form into 1-inch meatballs.

6. In a medium skillet, heat the olive oil over medium heat. Brown the meatballs on each side until cooked through, 3 to 5 minutes total. Use a slotted spoon to transfer them to the sauce.

7. Inside the spaghetti squash shell halves, layer the meatballs and sauce between layers of mozzarella cheese and spaghetti squash, finishing with a layer of mozzarella.

8. Place the filled spaghetti squash halves on the baking sheet and bake for 30 minutes.

PER SERVING: CALORIES: 478, TOTAL FAT: 28G; SATURATED FAT: 14G; PROTEIN: 59G; CHOLESTEROL: 175MG; CARBOHYDRATES: 11G; FIBER: 1G; **NET CARBS: 10G**

FAT: 48% / CARBS: 8% / PROTEIN: 44%

MAKE IT PALEO *Although this recipe is ooey-gooey with cheese, it can be made without it, and it will taste just as good.*

ROSEMARY PESTO COWBOY RIBEYE

SERVES 4 / PREP TIME: 10 MINUTES, PLUS 40 MINUTES TO REST / COOK TIME: 15 MINUTES

1 tablespoon plus
a pinch sea salt

½ teaspoon coarsely
ground black pepper

1 teaspoon garlic powder

1 (2-pound) grass-fed
cowboy ribeye steak or
2 (1-pound) grass-fed
boneless ribeyes

6 fresh rosemary
sprigs, divided

7 garlic cloves,
peeled, divided

1 tablespoon extra-virgin
olive oil, plus additional
for drizzling

3 tablespoons salted
grass-fed butter, at
room temperature

Get yer jeans on, yer spurs polished, and yer boots broken in, pardner! A cowboy ribeye isn't the cheapest cut of meat behind the butcher's counter, but when prepared well, it's the steak that beats out a tiny little filet mignon every single time. This cowboy ribeye is topped with a rosemary pesto butter, taking its flavor from here to the moon.

1. Preheat the oven to 400°F.

2. In a small bowl, combine the salt, pepper, and garlic powder. Rub both sides of the ribeye with this mixture. Let the meat rest on a plate on the counter for 30 minutes.

3. Put 5 rosemary sprigs and 5 garlic cloves in a cast iron skillet. Drizzle some olive oil over them so there's some in the bottom of the skillet. Place the ribeye on top of the rosemary and garlic so the steak does not touch the bottom of the skillet. Put the skillet in the oven and cook the meat to just before your desired doneness. It will take about 15 minutes to reach medium. Remove the skillet from the oven.

4. In a separate large skillet, warm 1 tablespoon of olive oil over high heat. Transfer the steak to that skillet and sear the steak on both sides, about 30 seconds per side. Place the seared steak on a plate and let rest for 10 minutes.

5. In a small bowl, combine the butter, a pinch of salt, the leaves of the remaining rosemary sprig, and the remaining 2 garlic cloves. Mash into a pesto.

6. Spread the pesto over the top of the steak and serve.

MAKE IT PALEO *Replace the butter with 1 tablespoon of ghee and add another pinch of salt.*

PER SERVING: CALORIES: 426; TOTAL FAT: 24G; SATURATED FAT: 11G; PROTEIN: 50G; CHOLESTEROL: 133MG; CARBOHYDRATES: 2G; FIBER: 0G; **NET CARBS: 2G**

FAT: 51% / CARBS: 2% / PROTEIN: 47%

COCONUT-LIME SKIRT STEAK

SERVES 2 TO 3 / PREP TIME: 10 MINUTES, PLUS 20 MINUTES TO MARINATE / COOK TIME: 10 MINUTES

¼ cup coconut oil, melted

2 tablespoons freshly squeezed lime juice

Grated zest of 1 lime

1 tablespoon minced garlic

1 teaspoon grated fresh ginger

1 teaspoon red pepper flakes

1 teaspoon sea salt

1 (2-pound) grass-fed skirt steak

Drawing from Thai flavors with the benefits of coconut oil, this lime and coconut infusion is dressed with red pepper flakes and brings a balance of sweet and spicy to ordinary skirt steak.

1. In a large bowl, combine the coconut oil, lime juice and zest, garlic, ginger, red pepper flakes, and salt. Add the steak and toss to coat it in the marinade. Let the meat marinate for 20 minutes at room temperature.

2. Transfer the steak to a large skillet set over medium-high heat. If it won't fit lengthwise, cut it in half against the grain. Sear the steak on both sides until it is cooked to your desired doneness, 4 to 5 minutes per side. Slice and serve.

PER SERVING: CALORIES: 1,182; TOTAL FAT: 73G; SATURATED FAT: 41G; PROTEIN: 121G; CHOLESTEROL: 268MG; CARBOHYDRATES: 4G; FIBER: 1G; **NET CARBS: 3G**

FAT: 56% / CARBS: 3% / PROTEIN: 41%

ROSEMARY-CHILI–CRUSTED NEW YORK STRIP

SERVES 4 / PREP TIME: 5 MINUTES / COOK TIME: 10 MINUTES

If you're making dinner for a hot date, show them a little romance with fragrant, earthy rosemary, and surprise them with the spice of chili at the end of the tongue.

1. In a small bowl, combine the ghee, garlic, rosemary, salt, pepper, and chili powder. Rub the mixture into both steaks.

2. In a cast iron skillet, sear the steaks over medium heat on each side, about 5 minutes per side, or until they reach your desired doneness.

3. Plate the steaks and let them rest for 5 minutes. Drizzle any ghee mixture from the pan over the steaks before serving.

PER SERVING: CALORIES: 395; TOTAL FAT: 21G; SATURATED FAT: 11G; PROTEIN: 51G; CHOLESTEROL: 146MG; CARBOHYDRATES: 1G; FIBER: 0G; **NET CARBS: 1G**

FAT: 48% / CARBS: 1% / PROTEIN: 51%

¼ cup Golden Ghee (page 224), melted

1 teaspoon minced garlic

Leaves from 2 rosemary sprigs

2 teaspoons sea salt

1 teaspoon freshly ground black pepper

⅛ teaspoon chili powder

2 (1-pound) grass-fed New York strip steaks

RECIPE TIP *If you can find it, try using pink Himalayan salt instead of sea salt. Pink Himalayan salt, considered the purest in the world, contains minerals like sulfate, magnesium, calcium, and potassium. I use it whenever possible.*

BLUE CHEESE BEEF ROLL-UPS

SERVES 4 / PREP TIME: 15 MINUTES, PLUS 30 MINUTES TO MARINATE / COOK TIME: 20 MINUTES

1 tablespoon extra-virgin olive oil

2 teaspoons minced garlic

2 teaspoons chopped fresh thyme leaves

2 teaspoons chopped fresh rosemary leaves

1 teaspoon sea salt

1 teaspoon freshly ground black pepper

⅛ teaspoon ground cinnamon

2 pounds grass-fed flank steak, pounded thin and cut into 4-by-4-inch pieces

½ cup crumbled organic blue cheese

Herb-infused grass-fed beef gives the strong blue cheese a warm hug in this dish, which can be served as an appetizer or a full meal. It's also great on top of romaine lettuce with blue cheese dressing.

1. Preheat the oven to 375°F.

2. Line a rimmed baking sheet with parchment paper. Soak 10 to 20 wooden toothpicks in water.

3. Meanwhile, combine the olive oil, garlic, thyme, rosemary, salt, pepper, and cinnamon in a zipper-top plastic bag. Add the steak and marinate for 30 minutes.

4. Lay out the steak pieces on the baking sheet in a single layer. Put some blue cheese in the middle of each, then roll up the beef and use a damp tooth-pick to secure each roll.

5. Bake until the meat reaches your desired doneness, 10 to 20 minutes. Serve.

PER SERVING: CALORIES: 527; TOTAL FAT: 27G; SATURATED FAT: 11G; PROTEIN: 66G; CHOLESTEROL: 136MG; CARBOHYDRATES: 2G; FIBER: 1G; **NET CARBS: 1G**

FAT: 46% / CARBS: 4% / PROTEIN: 50%

FLANK STEAK PIZZAIOLA PINWHEELS

SERVES 2 / PREP TIME: 10 MINUTES / COOK TIME: 20 MINUTES

Pizzaiola is what turns an ordinary steak into an Italian feast. Flank steak is a perfect cut to pound thin and then fill with fresh caprese-style cheeses and herbs like mozzarella and garden-picked basil.

1. Preheat the oven to 375°F.

2. Line a rimmed baking sheet with parchment paper.

3. In a medium bowl, mix the olive oil, Italian seasoning, garlic powder, salt, and pepper. Add the steak and toss well to coat with the mixture. Place the steak on the baking sheet.

4. In a medium microwave-safe bowl, heat the mozzarella on low for 30 seconds and then in 15-second intervals until it's pliable enough to work with. Add the basil and garlic-infused olive oil to the mozzarella. Heat it for another 15 seconds if necessary so it can be mixed together.

5. Spread the cheese mixture down the center of the flank steak, then roll up the steak, leaving it seam-side down on the parchment.

6. Bake until the steak reaches your desired doneness, 10 to 20 minutes. Slice the roll into pinwheels and serve topped with the marinara and Parmigiano-Reggiano cheese.

1 tablespoon extra-virgin olive oil

1 tablespoon Italian seasoning

2 teaspoons garlic powder

1 teaspoon sea salt

1 teaspoon freshly ground black pepper

1 pound grass-fed flank steak, pounded thin

1 (8-ounce) ball fresh organic mozzarella cheese

1 cup chopped fresh basil

2 tablespoons garlic-infused olive oil

½ cup Rhode Island Red Marinara Sauce (page 221), warmed

¼ cup shaved organic Parmigiano-Reggiano cheese, for serving

PER SERVING: CALORIES: 910; TOTAL FAT: 65G;
SATURATED FAT: 25G; PROTEIN: 73G; CHOLESTEROL: 210MG;
CARBOHYDRATES: 3G; FIBER: 1G; **NET CARBS: 2G**

FAT: 66% / CARBS: 1% / PROTEIN: 33%

SRIRACHA-CITRUS BEEF

SERVES 4 / PREP TIME: 10 MINUTES / COOK TIME: 10 MINUTES

1 tablespoon toasted sesame oil

2 pounds grass-fed flank steak, cut into thin strips

1 red bell pepper, seeded and cut into thin strips

1 tablespoon minced garlic

Juice of 1 small mandarin orange

3 tablespoons tamari

2 tablespoons sriracha

1 teaspoon rice vinegar

1 teaspoon sesame seeds

MAKE IT PALEO *The tamari can be omitted from this recipe, making it primarily a sriracha and orange–based dish.*

Just when you thought you had to give up oranges, I sneak in a mandarin orange. It's pleasantly keto-able when split by four people. The citrus in this Asian-inspired dish is balanced with a light touch of rice vinegar.

1. In a large skillet, heat the sesame oil over medium heat. When it is hot, add the steak, red bell pepper, and garlic, and cook until the steak is cooked through and the peppers are crisp-tender, about 3 minutes.

2. Stir in the orange juice, tamari, sriracha, and rice vinegar. Reduce the heat to low and simmer for 3 to 5 minutes.

3. Toss with the sesame seeds and serve.

PER SERVING: CALORIES: 503; TOTAL FAT: 23G; SATURATED FAT: 8G; PROTEIN: 65G; CHOLESTEROL: 125MG; CARBOHYDRATES: 5G; FIBER: 1G; **NET CARBS: 4G**

FAT: 41% / CARBS: 7% / PROTEIN: 52%

DIJON STEAK AND CHEESE-STUFFED PEPPERS

SERVES 4 / PREP TIME: 10 MINUTES / COOK TIME: 35 MINUTES

If you love a good steak and a good cheese, you'll be rolling on the floor in belly-filled happiness from these green pepper–infused Dijon mustard steak bombs.

1. Preheat the oven to 400°F.

2. Line a rimmed baking sheet with parchment paper.

3. Sit the green bell peppers, cut-side up, on the lined baking sheet. Chop the pepper tops.

4. In a large skillet, melt the ghee over medium-low heat. Add the chopped green pepper tops, onion, and garlic and cook until soft, about 2 minutes.

5. Add the olive oil to the skillet; when it is hot, add the steak. Cook until the meat is browned all the way through, about 2 minutes.

6. Reduce the heat to low. Stir in the mayonnaise and mustard.

7. Add two slices of American cheese on top of the steak and let it melt for about 1 minute. Stir to mix in the melted cheese throughout.

8. Spoon the steak mixture into the green peppers, and top each with a slice of American cheese. Bake until the green peppers are soft, about 30 minutes. Serve immediately.

4 green bell peppers, tops cut off and reserved, seeds and membranes removed

1 tablespoon Golden Ghee (page 224)

¼ cup chopped onion

1 tablespoon minced garlic

1 tablespoon extra-virgin olive oil or garlic-infused olive oil

1 pound shaved grass-fed steak

2 tablespoons mayonnaise

1 tablespoon Dijon mustard

6 slices organic American cheese, divided

PER SERVING: CALORIES: 433; TOTAL FAT: 25G;
SATURATED FAT: 10G; PROTEIN: 42G; CHOLESTEROL: 137MG;
CARBOHYDRATES: 9G; FIBER: 3G; **NET CARBS: 6G**

FAT: 53% / CARBS: 5% / PROTEIN: 42%

HERB-MARINATED SIRLOIN ROAST

SERVES 6 / PREP TIME: 10 MINUTES, PLUS OVERNIGHT TO MARINATE / COOK TIME: 1 HOUR

¼ cup extra-virgin olive oil

2 tablespoons Italian Dressing (page 227)

2 tablespoons minced garlic

¼ cup chopped fresh basil

¼ cup chopped fresh thyme leaves

2 tablespoons chopped fresh rosemary leaves

1 tablespoon sea salt

1 teaspoon coarsely ground black pepper

1 (3-pound) grass-fed sirloin roast

RECIPE TIP *Turn this into a slow cooker meal. Instead of marinating the meat, simply rub the marinade all over the roast and then cook it on low for 8 hours or on high for about 2 hours.*

Salt and olive oil make everything taste better. The more, usually, the better. I feel the same way about a good marinade, which should be rich and concentrated in its flavors for the best infusion.

1. In a large container with a lid, combine the olive oil, Italian dressing, garlic, basil, thyme, rosemary, salt, and pepper. Add the roast and turn it to coat. Marinate the roast overnight in the refrigerator.

2. Preheat the oven to 350°F.

3. Place the meat in a shallow roasting pan and bake until its internal temperature reaches 145°F, about 1 hour. Let the roast rest for 10 minutes before slicing.

PER SERVING: CALORIES: 590; TOTAL FAT: 43G; SATURATED FAT: 16G; PROTEIN: 47G; CHOLESTEROL: 124MG; CARBOHYDRATES: 4G; FIBER: 1G; **NET CARBS: 3G**

FAT: 66% / CARBS: 2% / PROTEIN: 32%

24-HOUR SPICY BEEF STEW

SERVES 6 TO 8 / PREP TIME: 10 MINUTES / COOK TIME: 24 HOURS

Winter is all about a hearty beef stew, but it's typically filled with carby potatoes and sugary carrots. This version drills down to a spicy, savory tomato broth and lets the marinated beef roast take center stage.

1. In the evening, turn on your slow cooker to low heat.

2. Rub the beef with the ranch rub. Place it in the slow cooker, cover, and cook it for 12 hours, until the beef falls apart.

3. In the morning, use two forks to shred the meat, and remove any excess hard fat that hasn't melted away.

4. Add the broth, ghee, hot sauce, both tomatoes with their juices, onion, garlic, and red pepper flakes to the slow cooker. Cook on low for another 12 hours. Serve.

PER SERVING: CALORIES: 208; TOTAL FAT: 16G; SATURATED FAT: 7G; PROTEIN: 11G; CHOLESTEROL: 36MG; CARBOHYDRATES: 3G; FIBER: 1G; **NET CARBS: 2G**

FAT: 72% / CARBS: 6% / PROTEIN: 22%

1 (3-pound) grass-fed pot roast

1 tablespoon Tangy Ranch Rub (page 219)

3 cups organic beef broth

1 tablespoon Golden Ghee (page 224)

2 teaspoons hot sauce, or more to taste

1 (10-ounce) can RO*TEL diced tomatoes and green chiles, undrained

1 (28-ounce) can diced tomatoes, undrained

½ medium onion, chopped

1 teaspoon minced garlic

½ teaspoon red pepper flakes

TRI-TIP GINGER-LIME STEAK KEBABS WITH MUSHROOMS AND RED PEPPERS

SERVES 4 / PREP TIME: 10 MINUTES, PLUS 1 HOUR TO MARINATE / COOK TIME: 10 MINUTES

2 tablespoons toasted sesame oil

1 tablespoon tamari

1 tablespoon freshly squeezed lime juice

1 teaspoon garlic salt

½ teaspoon ground ginger

½ teaspoon ground cumin

1 (2-pound) grass-fed tri-tip steak, cut into 2-inch cubes

2 cups halved white button mushrooms

2 red bell peppers, seeded and cut into squares

KETO TIP *Much of the carb count here is in the marinade, not the dish itself.*

Tri-tip can be as tender as ribeye, for the cost of sirloin (or less). Cut it into 2-inch cubes and dress it in this ginger-lime marinade. It's perfect for a cookout.

1. In a large bowl, whisk together the sesame oil, tamari, lime juice, garlic salt, ginger, and cumin. Add the tri-tip, mushrooms, and red peppers. Toss well and set aside to marinate for 1 hour. Meanwhile, soak 8 bamboo skewers in water for 1 hour.

2. Preheat your grill for high heat.

3. Skewer the marinated steak cubes between the mushrooms and red peppers.

4. Grill the kebabs for about 5 minutes on each side. Serve on or off the skewer.

PER SERVING: CALORIES: 508; TOTAL FAT: 26G; SATURATED FAT: 8G; PROTEIN: 63G; CHOLESTEROL: 161MG; CARBOHYDRATES: 7G; FIBER: 2G; **NET CARBS: 5G**

FAT: 46% / CARBS: 4% / PROTEIN: 50%

PAN-SEARED ROSEMARY-MINT LAMB LOLLIPOPS

SERVES 2 / PREP TIME: 10 MINUTES, PLUS 30 MINUTES TO MARINATE / COOK TIME: 5 MINUTES

Lamb is best served medium-rare, and you'll find it pairs well with fresh mint and fragrant rosemary for a tempting appetizer, or a whole meal.

1. In a large bowl, combine the olive oil, mint, rosemary, garlic, and garlic salt. Set about 1 tablespoon of the mixture aside.

2. Toss the lamb chops in the marinade remaining in the bowl. Cover the bowl with plastic wrap and refrigerate for 30 minutes.

3. In a cast iron skillet, cook the lamb lollipops over medium-high heat, about 2 minutes on each side for medium-rare.

4. Rest the chops on a plate for a couple of minutes, then drizzle with the reserved tablespoon of marinade and serve.

¼ cup extra-virgin olive oil

¼ cup chopped fresh mint

1 tablespoon chopped fresh rosemary leaves

1 tablespoon minced garlic

1 teaspoon garlic salt

8 grass-fed lamb rib chops

PER SERVING: CALORIES: 566; TOTAL FAT: 40G;
SATURATED FAT: 8G; PROTEIN: 47G; CHOLESTEROL: 147MG;
CARBOHYDRATES: 4G; FIBER: 2G; **NET CARBS: 2G**

FAT: 64% / CARBS: 3% / PROTEIN: 33%

CHAPTER EIGHT

PORK

SAUSAGE AND KALE CREAM SOUP

SERVES 4 TO 6 / PREP TIME: 10 MINUTES / COOK TIME: 20 MINUTES

1 pound organic bulk Italian sausage

½ cup chopped pancetta

½ cup chopped onion

2 cups organic heavy (whipping) cream

2 cups organic chicken broth

1 tablespoon minced garlic

½ teaspoon red pepper flakes

½ teaspoon freshly ground black pepper

½ teaspoon Italian seasoning

Sea salt (optional)

2 cups chopped kale

Spicy soups seem most appropriate on chilly winter days, and this light, creamy soup has just enough spice to draw you inside and keep you there.

1. In a large pot, sauté the Italian sausage, pancetta, and onion over medium heat until cooked through, about 5 minutes.

2. Stir in the heavy cream, chicken broth, garlic, red pepper flakes, black pepper, and Italian seasoning. Bring the soup to a boil, then reduce the heat to a simmer. Season the soup with salt (if using), and let it simmer for 10 minutes.

3. Stir in the kale and simmer for 5 more minutes.

PER SERVING: CALORIES: 470; TOTAL FAT: 45G; SATURATED FAT: 30G; PROTEIN: 4G; CHOLESTEROL: 154MG; CARBOHYDRATES: 3G; FIBER: 0G; **NET CARBS: 3G**

FAT: 94% / CARBS: 3% / PROTEIN: 3%

PORK-STUFFED BANANA PEPPERS

SERVES 2 / PREP TIME: 10 MINUTES / COOK TIME: 30 MINUTES

Sausage and banana peppers are two of my favorite pizza toppings. In this deconstructed version, banana peppers are the boats to float herbes de Provence–spiced sweet sausage down a river of tomato sauce with little mozzarella hats.

1. Preheat the oven to 350°F.

2. Line a rimmed baking sheet with parchment paper.

3. Brush the peppers with olive oil and place them on the sheet. Bake for 20 minutes.

4. Meanwhile, in a medium skillet, sauté the pork over medium heat until cooked through, stirring to break up any clumps, about 5 minutes. Mix in the onion, ghee, herbes de Provence, sage, marjoram, and red pepper flakes. Reduce the heat to low and cook for 5 minutes.

5. Remove the banana peppers from the oven and set the oven to broil.

6. Fill the banana peppers with the pork mixture. Top each with a bit of mozzarella cheese.

7. Pour the marinara sauce into the bottom of a small baking dish. Place the stuffed peppers on top of the marinara. Broil the peppers until the mozzarella is hot and bubbling, 5 to 10 minutes. Serve hot.

4 banana peppers, trimmed and butterflied into little boats

Extra-virgin olive oil

1 pound free-range ground pork

3 tablespoons chopped yellow onion

1 tablespoon Golden Ghee (page 224)

½ teaspoon herbes de Provence

1 teaspoon dried sage

¾ teaspoon dried marjoram

½ teaspoon red pepper flakes

½ cup shredded organic mozzarella cheese

1 cup Rhode Island Red Marinara Sauce (page 221)

PER SERVING: CALORIES: 740; TOTAL FAT: 38G; SATURATED FAT: 19G; PROTEIN: 70G; CHOLESTEROL: 211MG; CARBOHYDRATES: 12G; FIBER: 5G; **NET CARBS: 7G**

FAT: 51% / CARBS: 7% / PROTEIN: 42%

CHORIZO-STUFFED RED PEPPERS

SERVES 4 / PREP TIME: 10 MINUTES / COOK TIME: 40 MINUTES

4 red bell peppers,
tops cut off, seeds and
membranes removed

1 tablespoon extra-virgin
olive oil

¼ cup chopped onion

1 pound bulk
Mexican chorizo

½ teaspoon freshly
ground black pepper

½ teaspoon ground cumin

¼ teaspoon
ground paprika

¼ cup roughly chopped
fresh cilantro

1 cup shredded organic
Cheddar cheese, divided

INGREDIENT TIP *There are
two types of chorizo. The
Mexican version is uncured,
spiced ground meat, whereas
the Spanish chorizo is dried,
cured, and usually sold in
a casing.*

*Spicy chorizo infused with onion, cumin, and paprika
is tossed in a parade of cilantro leaves and baked in a
red bell pepper. Comfort food at its best.*

1. Preheat the oven to 400°F.

2. Line a rimmed baking sheet with parchment paper.

3. Sit the red bell peppers, cut-side up, on the
   baking sheet.

4. In a large skillet, heat the olive oil over
   medium-low heat. When it is hot, add the onion
   and cook until soft, about 3 minutes.

5. Add the chorizo, black pepper, cumin, and paprika
   and cook until the meat is browned and cooked all
   the way through, stirring to break up any clumps,
   about 5 minutes. Stir in the cilantro.

6. Spoon the chorizo mixture into the red bell peppers
   and top each with ¼ cup of Cheddar cheese.

7. Bake until the peppers are soft, about 30 minutes.
   Serve hot.

PER SERVING: CALORIES: 702; TOTAL FAT: 57G;
SATURATED FAT: 23G; PROTEIN: 36G; CHOLESTEROL: 129MG;
CARBOHYDRATES: 11G; FIBER: 3G; **NET CARBS: 8G**

FAT: 73% / CARBS: 6% / PROTEIN: 21%

SAGE SAUSAGE SCOTCH EGGS

SERVES 4 / PREP TIME: 10 MINUTES / COOK TIME: 15 MINUTES

A Scotch egg is a boiled egg encased in a layer of sausage flavored with sage and fennel. In the United Kingdom, Scotch eggs are as common as Buffalo wings at an American bar or a bagged pickle at the gas station. Unfortunately, the closest I've gotten to a Scotch egg here is the Rose & Crown at Epcot Center. Scotch eggs can be fried or baked; to make your life simple, here's the baked version.

1. Preheat the oven to 350°F.

2. Line two rimmed baking sheets with parchment paper.

3. In a large bowl, combine the pork, sage, fennel seed, nutmeg, marjoram, salt, and pepper. Use your hands to mix the ingredients together and form into 12 meatballs. Place the meatballs on the lined baking sheets and flatten them out.

4. Place one hardboiled egg in the middle of each flattened meatball and wrap the meat around each egg, leaving no gaps or holes.

5. Bake until the sausage is cooked through, about 15 minutes. Serve hot. Leftovers refrigerate very well.

2 pounds free-range ground pork

2 teaspoons chopped fresh sage leaves

1 teaspoon fennel seed

½ teaspoon grated fresh nutmeg

¼ teaspoon dried marjoram

2 teaspoons sea salt

1 teaspoon freshly ground black pepper

12 large free-range eggs, hardboiled and peeled

PER SERVING: CALORIES: 517; TOTAL FAT: 21G;
SATURATED FAT: 7G; PROTEIN: 76G; CHOLESTEROL: 657MG;
CARBOHYDRATES: 2G; FIBER: 0G; **NET CARBS: 2G**

FAT: 37% / CARBS: 4% / PROTEIN: 59%

SAUSAGE AND SAGE MEATLOAF WITH ORANGE ZEST

SERVES 4 / PREP TIME: 15 MINUTES / COOK TIME: 45 MINUTES

1 pound organic bulk sweet Italian sausage

2 cups crushed pork rinds

2 cups shredded organic mozzarella cheese

3 large free-range eggs, lightly beaten

⅓ cup organic heavy (whipping) cream

2 tablespoons Worcestershire sauce

½ yellow onion, chopped

4 large fresh sage leaves, chopped

½ teaspoon garlic powder

½ teaspoon onion powder

1 teaspoon sea salt

½ teaspoon freshly ground black pepper

2 tablespoons grated orange zest

Sweet and spicy sausage is married with earthy, fragrant sage in this meatloaf, which is topped with a tart orange zest.

1. Preheat the oven to 350°F.

2. In a large bowl, combine the sausage, pork rinds, mozzarella cheese, eggs, heavy cream, Worcestershire sauce, onion, sage, garlic powder, onion powder, salt, and pepper. Use your hands to mix the ingredients well. Evenly pack the meatloaf mixture into a 9-by-9-inch baking dish. Sprinkle the orange zest over the top of the meat.

3. Bake until cooked through, about 45 minutes. Let sit for 5 minutes, then slice and serve.

PER SERVING: CALORIES: 729; TOTAL FAT: 54G; SATURATED FAT: 23G; PROTEIN: 50G; CHOLESTEROL: 285MG; CARBOHYDRATES: 6G; FIBER: 1G; **NET CARBS: 5G**

FAT: 67% / CARBS: 5% / PROTEIN: 28%

DECONSTRUCTED EGG ROLL

SERVES 4 / PREP TIME: 10 MINUTES / COOK TIME: 15 MINUTES

An egg roll would be naturally ketogenic if it weren't for the wrapping. Here I take the best and most ketogenic parts of an eggroll, the pork and cabbage, to create a light, healthy meal bursting with Asian flavors.

1. In a medium skillet, brown the pork over medium heat until it is cooked through, stirring to break up any clumps, about 5 minutes.

2. Add the egg and scramble it until it is cooked through, about 1 minute.

3. Stir in the scallion, sesame seeds, tamari, sesame oil, rice wine, ginger, and a few grinds of pepper. Reduce the heat to low and simmer for 5 minutes.

4. Stir in the cabbage and cook until hot all the way through, about 3 minutes. Serve immediately.

PER SERVING: CALORIES: 250; TOTAL FAT: 10G;
SATURATED FAT: 2G; PROTEIN: 33G; CHOLESTEROL: 124MG;
CARBOHYDRATES: 7G; FIBER: 2G; **NET CARBS: 5G**

FAT: 36% / CARBS: 10% / PROTEIN: 54%

1 pound free-range ground pork

1 large free-range egg, beaten

3 tablespoons chopped scallion

1 tablespoon sesame seeds

1 tablespoon tamari

1 tablespoon toasted sesame oil

1 tablespoon Chinese rice wine

1 teaspoon ground ginger

Freshly ground black pepper

4 cups shredded cabbage

PORK AND GREEN BEAN ALFREDO CASSEROLE

SERVES 4 / PREP TIME: 10 MINUTES / COOK TIME: 40 MINUTES

- 1 tablespoon extra-virgin olive oil
- ½ white onion, chopped
- 1 pound free-range ground pork
- Pinch sea salt
- Pinch freshly ground black pepper
- 1 (8-ounce) package organic cream cheese, at room temperature
- 1 cup organic heavy (whipping) cream
- ¼ cup Golden Ghee (page 224), melted
- 2 tablespoons minced garlic
- ½ teaspoon garlic salt
- ½ teaspoon freshly ground white pepper
- ¼ cup grated organic Parmesan cheese
- 4 cups trimmed green beans
- 2 cups shredded organic Cheddar cheese

This casserole is easy to toss together, but it feels like a special occasion. Sweet green beans are high in fiber; here they are tossed in a rich cream cheese Alfredo sauce on top of a savory pork base.

1. Preheat the oven to 350°F.

2. In a medium skillet, heat the olive oil over medium heat. When it is hot, add the onion and cook until soft, about 3 minutes. Add the pork, salt, and black pepper to the pan. Brown the sausage until cooked through, stirring to break up any clumps, about 5 minutes.

3. Meanwhile, in a medium bowl, whisk the cream cheese, heavy cream, and ghee into a light cream sauce. If necessary, microwave the sauce in 15-second intervals to achieve a smooth consistency. Stir in the garlic, garlic salt, and white pepper. Then stir in the Parmesan cheese. Add the green beans to the bowl and toss to coat them with the sauce.

4. Transfer the cooked pork to a baking dish and top it with the green beans and sauce. Sprinkle the Cheddar cheese over the top.

5. Bake for 30 minutes. Serve hot.

PER SERVING: CALORIES: 904; TOTAL FAT: 73G; SATURATED FAT: 42G; PROTEIN: 54G; CHOLESTEROL: 283MG; CARBOHYDRATES: 12G; FIBER: 4G; **NET CARBS: 8G**

FAT: 73% / CARBS: 3% / PROTEIN: 24%

SAUSAGE AND PEPPER RAGOUT

SERVES 4 / PREP TIME: 5 MINUTES / COOK TIME: 40 MINUTES

This spicy, meaty sauce can be served over just about anything, but it's especially captivating over lightly sautéed zucchini noodles.

1. In a medium saucepan, bring the marinara to a simmer over medium heat.

2. In a medium skillet, brown the sausage over medium heat until cooked through, stirring to break up any clumps, about 5 minutes. Use a slotted spoon to add the meat to the marinara.

3. Add the green bell pepper to the skillet and cook it in the fat rendered from the sausage until soft, about 3 minutes. Stir it into the marinara.

4. Cover the marinara pot, reduce the heat to low, and simmer for 30 minutes. Serve.

2 cups Rhode Island Red Marinara Sauce (page 221)

1 pound organic bulk sausage

1 cup chopped green bell pepper

PER SERVING: CALORIES: 422; TOTAL FAT: 34G; SATURATED FAT: 11G; PROTEIN: 23G; CHOLESTEROL: 98MG; CARBOHYDRATES: 5G; FIBER: 1G; **NET CARBS: 4G**

FAT: 73% / CARBS: 4% / PROTEIN: 23%

PORKY PIG DINNER FRITTATA

SERVES 2 / PREP TIME: 10 MINUTES / COOK TIME: 30 MINUTES

8 ounces uncured center-cut bacon

8 ounces organic bulk sausage

4 ounces bulk Mexican chorizo

8 large free-range eggs

½ cup organic heavy (whipping) cream

⅓ cup shredded organic Cheddar cheese

2 teaspoons chopped fresh sage leaves

½ teaspoon sea salt

¼ teaspoon freshly ground black pepper

Salty bacon, savory sauce, and spicy Mexican chorizo come together for a dinner dance that celebrates every angle of pork, dressed in eggs.

1. Preheat the oven to 350°F.

2. Heat a 10-inch ovenproof skillet over medium-high heat. Add the bacon and cook until crispy, 3 to 4 minutes per side. Remove the bacon and set aside to cool.

3. Add the sausage and chorizo to the bacon fat left in the skillet and cook until browned, stirring to break up any clumps, about 5 minutes. Remove the meat with a slotted spoon and set aside to cool.

4. In a medium bowl, gently beat the eggs. Crumble the bacon into the bowl, then add the sausage and chorizo, heavy cream, Cheddar cheese, sage, salt, and pepper. Pour the egg mixture into the skillet.

5. Bake until the eggs are set and the top is golden brown, about 18 minutes. Let the frittata sit for a few minutes before slicing.

PER SERVING: CALORIES: 1,010; TOTAL FAT: 83G; SATURATED FAT: 34G; PROTEIN: 67G; CHOLESTEROL: 851MG; CARBOHYDRATES: 2G; FIBER: 0G; **NET CARBS: 2G**

FAT: 74% / CARBS: 1% / PROTEIN: 25%

BACON-RANCH QUESADILLA WITH CHICKEN

SERVES 2 / PREP TIME: 10 MINUTES / COOK TIME: 40 MINUTES

Salty bacon and creamy ranch dressing are the perfect complements to grilled chicken. In this recipe, bacon is the star. After all, everything is better with bacon.

20 uncured center-cut bacon strips

2 cups sliced grilled free-range chicken

¼ cup ranch dressing

½ cup shredded organic Cheddar cheese

1. Preheat the oven to 400°F.

2. Line a rimmed baking sheet with parchment paper.

3. Lay out 5 strips of bacon right next to each other on the sheet. One by one, weave the next 5 bacon strips into the first layer in the opposite direction, creating a woven bacon square. Repeat this with the remaining 10 bacon strips to make a second woven bacon square next to the first. Bake for 30 minutes.

4. Trim the bacon squares so they are about the same shape and size. Crumble any trimmed bacon and save for another recipe.

5. Layer the grilled chicken over one bacon square, drizzle it with the ranch dressing, and sprinkle with the Cheddar cheese. Top with the second bacon square.

6. Discard the used parchment and line the baking sheet with a new piece. Bake the quesadilla until the cheese melts, 5 to 10 minutes. Cut in half and serve.

PER SERVING: CALORIES: 619; TOTAL FAT: 35G; SATURATED FAT: 14G; PROTEIN: 79G; CHOLESTEROL: 233MG; CARBOHYDRATES: 2G; FIBER: 0G; **NET CARBS: 2G**

FAT: 51% / CARBS: 2% / PROTEIN: 47%

BACON MOZZARELLA STICKS

SERVES 3 / PREP TIME: 10 MINUTES, PLUS 1 HOUR TO FREEZE / COOK TIME: 15 MINUTES

6 whole-milk organic mozzarella cheese sticks

12 uncured center-cut bacon strips

Although I love a good crushed pork rind in Mini Mozzarella Sticks (page 72), did you know that bacon is basically the duct tape of keto? You can wrap anything with it, including mozzarella sticks. These are best served with blue cheese or ranch dressing.

1. Line a rimmed baking sheet with parchment paper. Place the cheese sticks on the sheet. Freeze for at least 1 hour.

2. Preheat the oven to 400°F.

3. Wrap each cheese stick in two strips of bacon—one strip lengthwise, and the other all the way around.

4. Bake for 15 minutes. Serve hot.

PER SERVING: CALORIES: 260; TOTAL FAT: 18G; SATURATED FAT: 9G; PROTEIN: 26G; CHOLESTEROL: 60MG; CARBOHYDRATES: 0G; FIBER: 0G; **NET CARBS: 0G**

FAT: 62% / CARBS: 0% / PROTEIN: 38%

BLACK PEPPER BACON JERKY

SERVES 6 / PREP TIME: 10 MINUTES / COOK TIME: 2 HOURS

Bacon can be its own meal when sprinkled with this savory and spicy dust before baking in the oven. It's also the perfect snack when you're on the go.

1. Preheat the oven to its lowest setting, likely between 150°F and 175°F.

2. In a large bowl, mix the garlic powder, cumin, paprika, chili powder, and pepper. Add the bacon strips to the bowl and coat them all over with the rub.

3. Place a few baking sheets on the bottom rack of the oven to catch any fat that renders from the bacon as it bakes. Lay the bacon directly on the top rack of the oven.

4. Bake for at least 2 hours; remove the bacon when it reaches your desired jerkiness.

1 tablespoon garlic powder

1 tablespoon ground cumin

1 tablespoon smoked paprika

1 tablespoon chili powder

1½ teaspoons freshly ground black pepper

1 pound uncured center-cut bacon

PER SERVING: CALORIES: 95; TOTAL FAT: 7G;
SATURATED FAT: 2G; PROTEIN: 9G; CHOLESTEROL: 23MG;
CARBOHYDRATES: 0G; FIBER: 0G; **NET CARBS: 0G**

FAT: 64% / CARBS: 0% / PROTEIN: 36%

BACON AND LEEK DINNER FRITTATA

SERVES 2 / PREP TIME: 10 MINUTES / COOK TIME: 25 MINUTES

8 ounces uncured center-cut bacon

¼ cup sliced leek (white part only)

8 large free-range eggs

½ cup organic heavy (whipping) cream

1 tablespoon freshly squeezed lemon juice

⅓ cup grated organic Parmesan cheese

2 teaspoons chopped fresh thyme leaves

½ teaspoon sea salt

¼ teaspoon freshly ground black pepper

Bacon and leeks pair brilliantly, as you get a mild onion flavor from the leek when it's roasted with salty, crispy bacon.

1. Preheat the oven to 350°F.

2. Place a 10-inch cast iron or ovenproof skillet over medium-high heat. When the pan is hot, add the bacon and cook until crispy, 3 to 4 minutes on each side. Remove the bacon and set aside to cool.

3. Add the leek to the bacon fat left in the pan and sauté for 3 minutes. Remove the leek from the pan and set aside to cool. Leave any remaining bacon fat in the pan.

4. In a medium bowl, gently beat the eggs, then whisk in the heavy cream, lemon juice, Parmesan cheese, thyme, salt, pepper, and cooled leek. Pour the egg mixture into the skillet and crumble the bacon over the top.

5. Bake until the eggs are set and the top is golden brown, about 18 minutes. Let the frittata sit for a few minutes before slicing.

PER SERVING: CALORIES: 575; TOTAL FAT: 44G; SATURATED FAT: 20G; PROTEIN: 46G; CHOLESTEROL: 751MG; CARBOHYDRATES: 4G; FIBER: 1G; **NET CARBS: 3G**

FAT: 68% / CARBS: 2% / PROTEIN: 30%

CHOCOLATE-COATED BACON

SERVES 6 / PREP TIME: 10 MINUTES / COOK TIME: 20 MINUTES

Salty, crispy bacon is dipped in buttery, melty chocolate for a sweet and savory treat that's neither breakfast, dinner, nor dessert—but somehow all three.

1. Preheat the oven to 400°F.

2. Line two rimmed baking sheets with parchment paper.

3. Lay out the bacon strips in a single layer on the sheets. Bake the bacon to your desired crispiness, 15 to 20 minutes (no need to flip the bacon midbake). Drain the bacon on paper towels.

4. In a small microwave-safe bowl, combine the ghee and chocolate. Microwave for three or four 15-second intervals, stirring between each interval, until the chocolate becomes soft and mixes easily with the ghee. Add the sweetener and heavy cream and mix until smooth.

5. Lay out the bacon on a fresh sheet of parchment paper on a baking sheet. Drizzle the chocolate over one-third of each bacon slice. Refrigerate the chocolate-coated bacon for about 5 minutes before serving.

1 pound uncured center-cut bacon

2 tablespoons Golden Ghee (page 224)

1 ounce unsweetened chocolate

1 tablespoon Sugar-Free Vanilla Bean Sweetener (page 196)

1 tablespoon organic heavy (whipping) cream

PER SERVING: CALORIES: 479; TOTAL FAT: 39G;
SATURATED FAT: 15G; PROTEIN: 30G; CHOLESTEROL: 98MG;
CARBOHYDRATES: 2G; FIBER: 1G; **NET CARBS: 1G**

FAT: 74% / CARBS: 1% / PROTEIN: 25%

WALNUT-CRUSTED PORK CHOPS

SERVES 2 / PREP TIME: 10 MINUTES / COOK TIME: 20 MINUTES

3 tablespoons
crushed walnuts

3 tablespoons grated
organic Parmesan cheese

Pinch sea salt

Pinch freshly ground
black pepper

1 large free-range egg

2 boneless free-range
pork chops

MAKE IT PALEO *Substitute
crushed pork rinds for the
Parmesan cheese.*

It's no secret that pork chops are the Harry Potter of the protein world (the Potter that still lived under the stairs, not the Potter that defeated Voldemort—that would be Maine lobster). But what I love about pork chops is that they're cheap, and with the right keto- genic "breading" you can take the flavor anywhere you want. Thick-cut pork chops work best because they stay juicy through the cooking process, but even with thin-cut chops you won't care about juic- iness because you'll be enjoying so much more of the delicious coating. Serve this over zoodles for a great meal.

1. Preheat the oven to 400°F.

2. Line a rimmed baking sheet with parchment paper.

3. In a shallow dish, mix the walnuts, Parmesan cheese, salt, and pepper.

4. In another shallow dish, lightly beat the egg.

5. One at a time, dip a pork chop in the egg, coat it with the walnut and Parmesan mixture, and place it on the baking sheet.

6. Bake the chops for 10 minutes, flip them, and continue baking until they reach 145°F in the center, about 10 minutes more. Serve immediately.

PER SERVING: CALORIES: 352; TOTAL FAT: 17G;
SATURATED FAT: 5G; PROTEIN: 47G; CHOLESTEROL: 195MG;
CARBOHYDRATES: 2G; FIBER: 1G; **NET CARBS: 1G**

FAT: 43% / CARBS: 4% / PROTEIN: 53%

SLOW COOKER RANCH PORK CHOPS

SERVES 4 / PREP TIME: 10 MINUTES / COOK TIME: 2½ HOURS

These thick-cut pork chops are coated in a dry ranch rub, then slow-cooked to juicy perfection. They're wonderful when served with a salad or wilted greens and garlic.

1. In a small bowl, stir together all the dry seasonings. You will use 1 tablespoon of rub for every 1 pound of pork in this recipe. Store any unused rub in an airtight container for later use.

2. Pour the broth into the slow cooker. Coat each pork chop with rub and place in the slow cooker.

3. Cover and cook on low until the internal temperature of the chops reaches 145°F, about 2½ hours. Serve hot.

PER SERVING: CALORIES: 494; TOTAL FAT: 36G;
SATURATED FAT: 13G; PROTEIN: 36G; CHOLESTEROL: 122MG;
CARBOHYDRATES: 5G; FIBER: 1G; **NET CARBS: 4G**

FAT: 66% / CARBS: 4% / PROTEIN: 30%

1 tablespoon plus
2 teaspoons onion powder

1 tablespoon plus
2 teaspoons dried parsley

1 tablespoon garlic salt

1 tablespoon
dried oregano

1 tablespoon sweet cream
buttermilk powder

2 teaspoons dried
dill weed

2 teaspoons garlic powder

2 teaspoons freshly
ground black pepper

1 teaspoon dried basil

¼ teaspoon dried thyme

¼ teaspoon celery salt

1 cup organic beef or
organic chicken broth

4 thick-cut boneless
free-range pork chops

ROASTED PORK CHOPS AND GARLIC GREEN BEANS

SERVES 4 / PREP TIME: 10 MINUTES / COOK TIME: 30 MINUTES

4 tablespoons garlic-infused olive oil, divided

4 thick-cut boneless free-range pork chops

2 cups trimmed green beans

10 garlic cloves, peeled

½ teaspoon garlic salt

5 fresh thyme sprigs

½ cup grated organic Parmesan cheese

½ cup freshly shaved organic Parmesan cheese

Garlic-infused olive oil should be a staple in any kitchen. It certainly is in mine. It comes in handy in recipes like this where the garlic acts as more of a side than a seasoning. After roasting in the oven, the garlic cloves turn into little pillows of creamy, garlicky lusciousness. You can eat them bite by bite, or make a Roasted Garlic Cream (page 231) to add to the green bean mixture.

1. Preheat the oven to 350°F.

2. In a large cast iron or ovenproof skillet, swirl 2 tablespoons of garlic-infused olive oil to coat the bottom. Add the pork chops. In between the chops and around the edges, distribute the green beans and garlic cloves. Drizzle the remaining 2 tablespoons of oil over the top of the meat and vegetables. Sprinkle with the garlic salt and place the thyme sprigs on top. Then sprinkle with the grated and shaved Parmesan cheese.

3. Bake until cooked through, about 30 minutes. Serve immediately.

PER SERVING: CALORIES: 694; TOTAL FAT: 55G; SATURATED FAT: 19G; PROTEIN: 45G; CHOLESTEROL: 142MG; CARBOHYDRATES: 6G; FIBER: 2G; **NET CARBS: 4G**

FAT: 71% / CARBS: 3% / PROTEIN: 26%

SPICED PULLED PORK

SERVES 10 / PREP TIME: 10 MINUTES / COOK TIME: 8 TO 12 HOURS

Pulled pork is so easy to make, especially if you have a slow cooker (and you should). Serve this slightly spicy dish with lime wedges and let your palate take a magic carpet ride to Austin, Texas—pulled pork dreamland.

1. Set the slow cooker to low. Pour in the broth and liquid smoke, and then add the onion slices. Place the pork butt on top of the onion slices.

2. In a small bowl, mix the paprika, chili powder, onion powder, garlic powder, salt, ground mustard, and cayenne pepper. Rub this mixture over the pork butt.

3. Cover and cook until the pork easily shreds with a fork, 8 to 12 hours. Transfer the pork to a large serving dish and use two forks to pull it apart.

4. In a blender, purée the juices and onions from the slow cooker.

5. Mix the sauce into the pulled pork and serve.

½ cup Lemon-Rosemary Bone Broth (page 193) or organic chicken broth

3 drops liquid smoke

½ onion, sliced

1 (3-pound) free-range pork butt

1 tablespoon paprika

1 tablespoon chili powder

1 tablespoon onion powder

1 tablespoon garlic powder

1 tablespoon sea salt

1 teaspoon ground mustard

1 teaspoon cayenne pepper

PER SERVING: CALORIES: 277; TOTAL FAT: 9G;
SATURATED FAT: 3G; PROTEIN: 43G; CHOLESTEROL: 125MG;
CARBOHYDRATES: 3G; FIBER: 1G; **NET CARBS: 2G**

FAT: 29% / CARBS: 9% / PROTEIN: 62%

LEMON-CAPER PORK FLORENTINE

SERVES 2 TO 4 / PREP TIME: 10 MINUTES / COOK TIME: 30 MINUTES

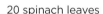

20 spinach leaves

8 boneless free-range pork cutlets

2 tablespoons drained capers

½ cup (1 stick) salted grass-fed butter

2 tablespoons chopped sweet white onion

2 garlic cloves, minced

4 teaspoons freshly squeezed lemon juice

4 teaspoons grated lemon zest

2 teaspoons chopped fresh parsley

As a kid I ate a lot of chicken Florentine but always felt that the chicken overpowered the delicate flavor of the sauce. Here, I've used thin pork cutlets, which are happy to let the lemon-caper sauce steal the show.

1. Preheat the oven to 375°F.
2. In a small baking dish, layer the spinach leaves between the pork cutlets, like fallen dominos, and scatter the capers over the pork and spinach.
3. In a small saucepan, melt the butter over low heat. Add the onion and garlic and cook until soft, stirring often so the butter does not brown, about 2 minutes. Whisk in the lemon juice and zest, and parsley. Pour the sauce over the pork cutlets.
4. Bake for 25 minutes. Serve hot.

PER SERVING: CALORIES: 587; TOTAL FAT: 50G; SATURATED FAT: 31G; PROTEIN: 31G; CHOLESTEROL: 205MG; CARBOHYDRATES: 4G; FIBER: 1G; **NET CARBS: 3G**

FAT: 77% / CARBS: 2% / PROTEIN: 21%

TUSCAN SPINACH AND HAVARTI–STUFFED PORK LOIN

SERVES 2 / PREP TIME: 20 MINUTES / COOK TIME: 45 MINUTES

This Havarti-slathered pork dish flavored with Tuscan herbs is juicy, delicious, and hard to share.

1. Preheat the oven to 400°F.

2. Grease a 13-by-9-inch baking dish with butter.

3. Butterfly the pork loin by cutting it lengthwise, but do not cut all the way through, just enough to open it like a book. Liberally brush the butterflied pork loin all over with the olive oil.

4. In a large bowl, mix the Parmesan cheese, sesame seeds, dried bell pepper, garlic powder, onion powder, and salt. Add the pork to the bowl and completely cover it inside and out with the mixture.

5. Place the pork loin in the baking dish and evenly spread any remaining herb mixture from the bowl on the loin. Arrange the spinach on one side of the pork, then layer the Havarti cheese over the spinach. Close the pork loin like a book, and wrap it with silicone baking bands or kitchen twine.

6. With a meat injector, inject the mustard into the pork loin at multiple points. Alternatively, just spread 1 teaspoon of mustard over the top of the pork loin.

7. Roast the pork until its internal temperature reads 145°F on a meat thermometer, about 45 minutes. Let it rest for 5 minutes before slicing.

Grass-fed butter, at room temperature

1 (1-pound) pork loin

¼ cup extra-virgin olive oil

½ cup grated organic Parmesan cheese

½ teaspoon toasted sesame seeds

½ teaspoon dried bell pepper

½ teaspoon garlic powder

½ teaspoon onion powder

½ teaspoon sea salt

1 cup fresh spinach leaves

1 (6- to 8-ounce) block organic garlic and herb Havarti cheese, sliced

1 tablespoon Dijon mustard

PER SERVING: CALORIES: 1,225; TOTAL FAT: 93G;
SATURATED FAT: 39G; PROTEIN: 95G; CHOLESTEROL: 298MG;
CARBOHYDRATES: 3G; FIBER: 1G; **NET CARBS: 2G**

FAT: 68% / CARBS: 2% / PROTEIN: 30%

CHAPTER NINE

CHICKEN

PROSCIUTTO-WRAPPED SMOKED GOUDA AND SPINACH CHICKEN

SERVES 2 / PREP TIME: 10 MINUTES / COOK TIME: 20 MINUTES

1 tablespoon extra-virgin olive oil

1 cup chopped fresh spinach

1 tablespoon minced garlic

½ cup shaved organic smoked Gouda

¼ cup grated organic Parmesan cheese

2 large boneless, skinless free-range chicken breasts, butterflied

4 large, thin slices prosciutto

MAKE IT PALEO *Nix the cheese, leave the garlic cloves whole (but peeled), and add a sprinkling of red pepper flakes to the spinach. Cover the skillet while the chicken bakes, and cook it a little longer so the garlic cloves roast inside the chicken.*

Prosciutto is a delightful alternative to bacon—lighter in flavor and better for wrapping chicken. Here, the crispy, salty pork completes the dish.

1. Preheat the oven to 400°F.

2. In a large cast iron or ovenproof skillet, swirl the olive oil to coat the bottom.

3. In a medium bowl, combine the spinach, minced garlic, and Gouda and Parmesan cheeses. Divide the spinach mixture between the two chicken breasts. Close each breast to envelop the spinach. Wrap each breast with 2 slices of prosciutto.

4. Place the breasts in the skillet and bake until the prosciutto is crispy and the internal temperature of the chicken reaches at least 165°F, about 20 minutes. Serve hot.

PER SERVING: CALORIES: 549; TOTAL FAT: 31G; SATURATED FAT: 11G; PROTEIN: 63G; CHOLESTEROL: 186MG; CARBOHYDRATES: 3G; FIBER: 0G; **NET CARBS: 3G**

FAT: 51% / CARBS: 3% / PROTEIN: 46%

PULLED BUFFALO CHICKEN SALAD WITH BLUE CHEESE

SERVES 2 / PREP TIME: 10 MINUTES / COOK TIME: 30 MINUTES

Chunky blue cheese and spicy buffalo sauce throw a victory party in your mouth when they come together in this refreshing salad.

2 boneless, skinless free-range chicken breasts

4 uncured center-cut bacon strips

¼ cup Buffalo Sauce (page 223)

4 cups chopped romaine lettuce, divided

½ cup blue cheese dressing, divided

½ cup crumbled organic blue cheese, divided

¼ cup chopped red onion, divided

1. Bring a large pot of water to a boil over high heat. Add the chicken breasts to the water, reduce the heat to low, and simmer the breasts until their internal temperature reaches 180°F, about 30 minutes. Transfer the chicken to a bowl and let it cool for about 10 minutes.

2. Meanwhile, crisp the bacon strips in a skillet over medium heat, about 3 minutes per side. Drain the bacon on a paper towel.

3. Use a fork to shred the chicken. Toss it with the buffalo sauce.

4. Divide the lettuce between two bowls. Top each with half of the pulled chicken, then half of the blue cheese dressing, blue cheese crumbles, and chopped red onion. Crumble the bacon over the salads and serve.

PER SERVING: CALORIES: 843; TOTAL FAT: 65G;
SATURATED FAT: 14G; PROTEIN: 59G; CHOLESTEROL: 156MG;
CARBOHYDRATES: 6G; FIBER: 1G; **NET CARBS: 5G**

FAT: 69% / CARBS: 2% / PROTEIN: 29%

RED PEPPER AND MOZZARELLA–STUFFED CHICKEN CAPRESE

SERVES 2 / PREP TIME: 10 MINUTES / COOK TIME: 40 MINUTES

10 fresh basil leaves

2 boneless, skinless
free-range chicken
breasts, butterflied

1 (8-ounce) ball fresh
organic mozzarella
cheese, cut into 4 pieces

1 cup Roasted Red
Peppers (page 235)

2 tablespoons
Italian seasoning

Sea salt

Freshly ground
black pepper

Mozzarella and red peppers make this dish slightly sweet but still high enough in fat for our keto-genic purposes.

1. Preheat the oven to 400°F.

2. Line a rimmed baking sheet with parchment paper.

3. Place 5 basil leaves inside each chicken breast.

4. Place 2 mozzarella slices inside each breast.

5. Divide the roasted red peppers between the two breasts. Sprinkle the Italian seasoning generously over each breast and season them with salt and pepper. Close each breast to envelop the filling.

6. Place the breasts on the baking sheet and bake until cooked through, about 40 minutes. Serve hot.

PER SERVING: CALORIES: 539; TOTAL FAT: 30G;
SATURATED FAT: 8G; PROTEIN: 63G; CHOLESTEROL: 152MG;
CARBOHYDRATES: 4G; FIBER: 1G; **NET CARBS: 3G**

FAT: 50% / CARBS: 3% / PROTEIN: 47%

LEMON-GARLIC CHICKEN AND GREEN BEANS WITH CARAMELIZED ONIONS

SERVES 2 / PREP TIME: 10 MINUTES, PLUS 1 HOUR TO MARINATE / COOK TIME: 65 MINUTES

Although it's not advisable to eat all the onion used here due to the high carb count, there's nothing wrong with infusing your whole dish with their flavor, and snagging some sweet and sticky caramelized ones at the end.

1. In a medium bowl or zipper-top plastic bag, mix the olive oil, lemon juice, garlic, salt, black pepper, paprika, and red pepper flakes. Add the chicken and coat it with the marinade. Cover the bowl or seal the bag and marinate the chicken in the refrigerator for at least 1 hour, or overnight if possible.

2. Preheat the oven to 350°F.

3. Dice one of the onion quarters, and cut the remaining three quarters into large chunks. Spread the larger chunks of onion across the bottom of a cast iron or ovenproof skillet. Add the green beans, and then scatter the diced onion on top. Top the green beans and onion with the ghee. Place the marinated chicken breasts on the green beans and spoon the remaining marinade over the chicken. Season the dish with a generous sprinkle of sea salt.

4. Bake the chicken until its internal temperature reaches at least 165°F, about 65 minutes. Serve hot.

3 tablespoons extra-virgin olive oil

3 tablespoons freshly squeezed lemon juice

2 tablespoons minced garlic

1 teaspoon sea salt, plus additional for seasoning

¼ teaspoon freshly ground black pepper

¼ teaspoon paprika

⅛ teaspoon red pepper flakes

2 large boneless, skinless free-range chicken breasts

1 yellow onion, quartered

2 cups trimmed green beans

¼ cup Golden Ghee (page 224), melted

PER SERVING: CALORIES: 803; TOTAL FAT: 61G;
SATURATED FAT: 23G; PROTEIN: 53G; CHOLESTEROL: 217MG;
CARBOHYDRATES: 14G; FIBER: 5G; **NET CARBS: 9G**

FAT: 69% / CARBS: 5% / PROTEIN: 26%

CHICKEN PARMESAN AND ZOODLES

SERVES 4 / PREP TIME: 10 MINUTES / COOK TIME: 45 MINUTES

2 cups crushed pork rinds

1 cup grated organic
Parmesan cheese

2 tablespoons
Italian seasoning

4 boneless, skinless
free-range chicken
breasts, butterflied
and pounded flat

1 cup shredded organic
mozzarella cheese

4 small to medium
zucchini

2 tablespoons garlic-
infused olive oil

1 teaspoon garlic salt

1 cup Rhode Island
Red Marinara Sauce
(page 221)

There's nothing like an old-fashioned Italian dinner with the family that consists of ridiculously sized slabs of breaded chicken and a big bowl of pasta. Of course, chicken Parmesan isn't exactly an authentic Italian dish, but we'll pretend it is for the sake of our eager taste buds. This recipe is an homage to the original—a perfectly cooked "breaded" breast on top of tender garlicky zoodles with stringy mozzarella cheese and homemade tomato sauce.

1. Preheat the oven to 375°F.

2. Line a rimmed baking sheet with parchment paper and set a wire rack on the parchment.

3. In a large bowl, combine the pork rinds, Parmesan cheese, and Italian seasoning. One at a time, put a chicken breast in the bowl and shake the bowl until the breast is totally covered in breading. Place each breaded chicken breast on the wire rack.

4. Sprinkle the mozzarella cheese on the top of each chicken breast.

5. Bake the chicken until cooked through, 30 to 45 minutes.

6. Meanwhile, spiralize the zucchini or shave them with a vegetable peeler. Place the zoodles in a large bowl and toss them with the garlic oil and garlic salt. Set aside.

7. When the chicken breasts are done, remove them from the oven and transfer to a serving plate.

8. In a large skillet, warm the seasoned zoodles over medium-high heat. Cook them just enough to get them hot, 1 to 2 minutes. Add the marinara and continue cooking only until the marinara is hot, about 1 more minute.

9. Plate the saucy zoodles next to the chicken, and drizzle any extra tomato sauce over the dish. Serve immediately.

PER SERVING: CALORIES: 519; TOTAL FAT: 27G;
SATURATED FAT: 12G; PROTEIN: 63G; CHOLESTEROL: 158MG;
CARBOHYDRATES: 10G; FIBER: 4G; **NET CARBS: 6G**

FAT: 47% / CARBS: 5% / PROTEIN: 48%

CREAMY RED PEPPER–STUFFED CHICKEN BREASTS

SERVES 4 / PREP TIME: 30 MINUTES / COOK TIME: 40 MINUTES

FOR THE CHICKEN

2 large boneless, skinless free-range chicken breasts, butterflied and pounded flat

2 tablespoons extra-virgin olive oil

1½ teaspoons Seasoned Salt (page 216)

½ teaspoon freshly ground black pepper

1 large red bell pepper, seeded and cut into thin strips

½ cup organic cream cheese, at room temperature

½ white onion, sliced

If you love sweet juicy red bell peppers, you'll love this infusion of tender chicken in a creamy red pepper sauce.

TO MAKE THE CHICKEN

1. Preheat the oven to 400°F.

2. Line a rimmed baking sheet with parchment paper.

3. Lay the butterflied chicken breasts flat on a work surface. Cover them with the olive oil, seasoned salt, and pepper.

4. Divide the red pepper strips, cream cheese, and onion slices between the chicken breasts, placing them down the center of each breast. Roll up the chicken breasts and place them on the lined baking sheet, seam-side down.

5. Bake until the chicken is cooked through, about 40 minutes.

TO MAKE THE SAUCE

1. Meanwhile, in a medium skillet, heat the ghee over medium heat. When it is hot, add the roasted red pepper, onion, and garlic and cook for 5 minutes. Stir in the heavy cream, red pepper flakes, salt, and black pepper and simmer, stirring frequently, until the sauce has reduced by half, about 10 minutes.

2. To serve, plate the cooked chicken and spoon the sauce over it.

PER SERVING: CALORIES: 417; TOTAL FAT: 29G; SATURATED FAT: 13G; PROTEIN: 28G; CHOLESTEROL: 126MG; CARBOHYDRATES: 8G; FIBER: 2G; **NET CARBS: 6G**

FAT: 65% / CARBS: 7% / PROTEIN: 28%

FOR THE SAUCE

1 tablespoon Golden Ghee (page 224)

1 large roasted red bell pepper, diced

½ white onion, diced

1 tablespoon minced garlic

¼ cup organic heavy (whipping) cream

⅛ teaspoon red pepper flakes

Pinch sea salt

Pinch freshly ground black pepper

THREE-CHEESE CHICKEN CORDON BLEU

SERVES 2 / PREP TIME: 10 MINUTES / COOK TIME: 50 MINUTES

½ cup shredded organic Gruyère cheese

½ cup shredded organic Emmentaler (Swiss) cheese

¼ cup shredded organic Appenzeller cheese

⅛ teaspoon ground nutmeg

2 large boneless, skinless, free-range chicken breasts, butterflied and pounded thin

4 slices nitrate-free ham

2 teaspoons Dijon mustard (optional)

1 tablespoon extra-virgin olive oil

½ cup grated organic Parmesan cheese

½ teaspoon Seasoned Salt (page 216)

Inspired by a traditional Swiss fondue, this chicken cordon bleu is singing from the Alps about its savory three-cheese blend with a dash of nutmeg, enveloping salty ham, which is, in turn, hugging a dash of tangy Dijon mustard.

1. Preheat the oven to 375°F.

2. Line a rimmed baking sheet with parchment paper.

3. In a small bowl, combine the Gruyère, Emmentaler, and Appenzeller cheeses with the nutmeg.

4. Lay the butterflied chicken breasts flat on a work surface and divide the cheese mixture between the two breasts.

5. Then place 2 slices of ham on top of the cheese on each breast, followed by 1 teaspoon of Dijon mustard in the middle (if using). Fold the chicken breast over to enclose the filling.

6. Brush the chicken with olive oil, then sprinkle it with the Parmesan cheese and seasoned salt.

7. Place the stuffed chicken breasts on the baking sheet and bake until the internal temperature reaches at least 165°F, about 50 minutes. Serve hot.

PER SERVING: CALORIES: 848; TOTAL FAT: 52G; SATURATED FAT: 23G; PROTEIN: 88G; CHOLESTEROL: 278MG; CARBOHYDRATES: 4G; FIBER: 1G; **NET CARBS: 3G**

FAT: 55% / CARBS: 3% / PROTEIN: 42%

CHICKEN AND BROCCOLI ALFREDO

SERVES 2 / PREP TIME: 10 MINUTES / COOK TIME: 25 MINUTES

Say good-bye to the pasta and let the chicken and broccoli soak up the lemony, peppery cream sauce. Feel free to add zucchini noodles.

1. Bring a large pot of water to a boil over high heat. Add the chicken breasts, making sure they are completely submerged. Reduce the heat to low and simmer, covered, until the chicken's internal temperature reaches 165°F, about 20 minutes. Remove the chicken and set aside.

2. Meanwhile, set a steamer rack inside a small saucepan and pour in just enough water to come to the bottom of the rack. Bring the water to a boil over high heat. Add the broccoli, cover the pot, and steam the broccoli until tender, about 6 minutes. Drain the broccoli and chop it into bite-size pieces.

3. In a medium skillet, heat the mascarpone, heavy cream, ghee, garlic, salt, and lemon pepper seasoning. Once the mixture is hot, reduce the heat to low and add the broccoli. Cook, stirring frequently, for 5 minutes.

4. In the meantime, use a fork to shred the chicken, discarding any tough fatty bits. Add the shredded chicken to the skillet and stir everything together until hot, about 2 minutes.

5. Divide the Alfredo between two plates, sprinkle with the Asiago cheese, and serve.

2 large boneless, skinless free-range chicken breasts

⅓ cup broccoli florets

⅓ cup organic mascarpone

3 tablespoons organic heavy (whipping) cream

2 tablespoons Golden Ghee (page 224)

2 teaspoons minced garlic

2 pinches sea salt

¼ teaspoon lemon pepper seasoning

2 tablespoons shaved organic Asiago cheese

PER SERVING: CALORIES: 632; TOTAL FAT: 44G; SATURATED FAT: 22G; PROTEIN: 58G; CHOLESTEROL: 245MG; CARBOHYDRATES: 2G; FIBER: 1G; **NET CARBS: 1G**

FAT: 63% / CARBS: 1% / PROTEIN: 36%

CHICKEN AND SPINACH RICOTTA CRÊPES

SERVES 2 / PREP TIME: 15 MINUTES / COOK TIME: 25 MINUTES

4 cups chopped
fresh spinach

¾ cup organic
ricotta cheese

⅓ cup grated organic
Parmesan cheese

¼ cup mayonnaise

1 tablespoon
minced garlic

¼ teaspoon sea salt

Pinch freshly ground
black pepper

Pinch red pepper flakes

Pinch nutmeg

2 large boneless, skinless
free-range chicken
breasts, butterflied
and pounded thin

Seasoned Salt (page 216)

Traditional crêpes are basically very thin pancakes filled with wonderful ingredients. This recipe borrows the same concept but uses big, juicy chicken breasts pounded into a thin layer to wrap around garlicky ricotta cheese and green leafy spinach.

1. Preheat the oven to 425°F.

2. Line a rimmed baking sheet with parchment paper.

3. In a large bowl, mix the spinach, ricotta and Parmesan cheeses, mayonnaise, garlic, salt, black pepper, red pepper flakes, and nutmeg.

4. Lay the butterflied chicken breasts flat on a work surface and divide the spinach mixture between the two breasts. Roll up each chicken breast and place it seam-side down on the baking sheet. Sprinkle the chicken with seasoned salt.

5. Bake until the internal temperature reaches 165°F, about 25 minutes. Serve hot.

PER SERVING: CALORIES: 677; TOTAL FAT: 39G;
SATURATED FAT: 14G; PROTEIN: 72G; CHOLESTEROL: 208MG;
CARBOHYDRATES: 9G; FIBER: 1G; **NET CARBS: 8G**

FAT: 50% / CARBS: 7% / PROTEIN: 43%

CREAMY SUN-DRIED TOMATO CHICKEN AND SAUSAGE

SERVES 4 / PREP TIME: 10 MINUTES / COOK TIME: 30 MINUTES

This dish gets its creaminess from the melted mozzarella, sweetness from the sun-dried tomatoes, and spiciness from red pepper flakes. Serve with a side of steamed veggies or over zucchini noodles.

💰 💰 💰

1 pound free-range chicken tenders

6 organic sausage links

¼ cup organic chicken broth

1 tablespoon Golden Ghee (page 224), melted

5 garlic cloves, peeled

5 sun-dried tomatoes

2 tablespoons chopped fresh basil leaves

1 tablespoon fresh thyme leaves

1 tablespoon chopped fresh oregano leaves

¼ teaspoon red pepper flakes

¾ cup organic heavy (whipping) cream

¾ cup shredded organic mozzarella cheese

¼ cup shredded organic Parmesan cheese

1. Preheat the oven to 350°F.
2. Place the chicken tenders and sausage links in one half of an ovenproof skillet. In the other half, combine the chicken broth, ghee, garlic cloves, and sun-dried tomatoes. Sprinkle everything with the basil, thyme, oregano, and red pepper flakes.
3. Bake until the chicken and sausages are cooked through, about 25 minutes.
4. Remove the chicken and sausages and cut them into bite-size pieces. Set aside.
5. Remove the sun-dried tomatoes and garlic and roughly chop them, then return them to the skillet.
6. Place the skillet over medium heat, stir in the heavy cream, and bring it to a simmer.
7. Add the mozzarella and Parmesan cheeses, a sprinkle at a time, until thoroughly melted, then mix in the sausage and chicken. If the mixture is too thick, add a tablespoon of chicken broth at a time until it reaches your desired consistency.
8. Once the chicken and sausage are warm, serve.

PER SERVING: CALORIES: 471; TOTAL FAT: 29G;
SATURATED FAT: 13G; PROTEIN: 49G; CHOLESTEROL: 167MG;
CARBOHYDRATES: 3G; FIBER: 1G; **NET CARBS: 2G**

FAT: 55% / CARBS: 2% / PROTEIN: 43%

PUMPKIN CURRY CHICKEN

SERVES 2 / PREP TIME: 10 MINUTES / COOK TIME: 15 MINUTES

7 ounces pure
pumpkin purée (not
pumpkin pie filling)

½ cup unsweetened
coconut milk

2 tablespoons Golden
Ghee (page 224)

1 tablespoon freshly
squeezed lime juice

½ small white
onion, chopped

2 tablespoons chopped
fresh Thai basil leaves

1 teaspoon curry powder

½ teaspoon ground
coriander

½ teaspoon ground
cinnamon

½ teaspoon ground ginger

½ teaspoon sea salt, plus
additional for seasoning

½ teaspoon red
pepper flakes

2 tablespoons extra-virgin
olive oil

1 pound free-range
chicken tenders

Freshly ground
black pepper

*On a cold day, there's nothing I love more than a bowl
of curry. What's even better are the leftovers; you'll
wake up to an even spicier version the next day, and
the next, and the next. Serve with zucchini noodles or
a side of steamed veggies.*

1. In a blender, combine the pumpkin, coconut milk,
   ghee, lime juice, onion, Thai basil, curry powder,
   coriander, cinnamon, ginger, salt, and red pepper
   flakes. Pour the mixture into a small saucepan set
   over medium heat.

2. In a medium skillet, heat the olive oil over medium
   heat. Season the chicken tenders with salt and
   black pepper. When the oil is hot, cook the chicken
   tenders until cooked through, about 3 minutes
   per side.

3. Cut the chicken into 1-inch pieces and add them
   to the pumpkin curry. Reduce the heat to low and
   cook for 5 to 10 minutes. Serve hot.

PER SERVING: CALORIES: 540; TOTAL FAT: 32G;
SATURATED FAT: 11G; PROTEIN: 54G; CHOLESTEROL: 163MG;
CARBOHYDRATES: 13G; FIBER: 6G; **NET CARBS: 7G**

FAT: 55% / CARBS: 5% / PROTEIN: 40%

BLACK PEPPER CHICKEN

SERVES 2 / PREP TIME: 10 MINUTES, PLUS 30 MINUTES TO MARINATE / COOK TIME: 25 MINUTES

If you've ever felt magnetically pulled to a high-end Chinese buffet, invariably the pot of gold was the black pepper chicken. It might be breaded or it might be grilled, but here we're going with baked.

1. In a medium bowl, whisk together the chicken broth, sake, oyster sauce, tamari, garlic, Creole seasoning, pepper, chili powder, and ginger.

2. Add the chicken, onion, and red bell pepper and toss to coat. Cover the bowl and marinate the chicken in the refrigerator for 30 minutes.

3. Preheat the oven to 350°F.

4. Transfer the chicken and marinade to a cast iron or ovenproof skillet. Bake the chicken until cooked through, mixing everything at least twice while in the oven, about 25 minutes.

PER SERVING: CALORIES: 422; TOTAL FAT: 10G; SATURATED FAT: 0G; PROTEIN: 76G; CHOLESTEROL: 194MG; CARBOHYDRATES: 6G; FIBER: 2G; **NET CARBS: 4G**

FAT: 21% / CARBS: 7% / PROTEIN: 72%

½ cup organic chicken broth

½ cup sake

3 tablespoons gluten-free oyster sauce

1 teaspoon tamari

2 garlic cloves, minced

1 tablespoon Creole seasoning

1 teaspoon freshly ground black pepper

1 teaspoon chili powder

1 teaspoon ground ginger

1 pound free-range chicken tenders, cut into 1-inch pieces

½ red onion, sliced

½ red bell pepper, cut into strips

KETO TIP *Oyster sauce almost always includes cornstarch, which strict paleo-ers and ketoers won't like. Find the purest, most natural version of oyster sauce you can.*

BUFFALO CHICKEN MEATLOAF STUFFED WITH BLUE CHEESE

SERVES 6 / PREP TIME: 15 MINUTES / COOK TIME: 1 HOUR

1 pound free-range ground chicken

½ cup crushed pork rinds

2 tablespoons almond flour

¼ cup chopped onion

1 tablespoon dried parsley

1½ teaspoons Old Bay Seasoning

1 cup crumbled organic blue cheese, plus additional for garnish

¼ cup chopped celery

¼ cup chopped carrots

1 cup Buffalo Sauce (page 223)

For buffalo chicken lovers, this is like a Super Bowl party in a tuxedo.

1. Preheat the oven to 375°F.

2. In a large bowl, combine the chicken, pork rinds, almond flour, onion, parsley, and Old Bay. Use your hands to mix the ingredients well.

3. Place the meatloaf mixture on a large piece of parchment paper. The mixture will be moist, but try to shape it into a large rectangle. Place the blue cheese, celery, and carrots in the middle of the rectangle. Lift one side of the parchment paper and use it to fold one side of the meatloaf over to its center. Do the same thing on the other side, thus covering the vegetables and cheese. Use the paper or your hands to smooth the meatloaf and close up the ends, fully sealing in the vegetables and cheese.

4. Transfer the parchment and meatloaf to a baking pan. Bake the meatloaf until it has cooked through and reaches an internal temperature of 180°F, about 1 hour.

5. Drizzle the buffalo sauce over the finished meatloaf and garnish with a sprinkle of blue cheese crumbles. Slice and serve.

PER SERVING: CALORIES: 364; TOTAL FAT: 27G; SATURATED FAT: 12G; PROTEIN: 27G; CHOLESTEROL: 115MG; CARBOHYDRATES: 3G; FIBER: 1G; **NET CARBS: 2G**

FAT: 67% / CARBS: 3% / PROTEIN: 30%

CHEESY CHICKEN PARMESAN MEATBALLS

SERVES 5 / PREP TIME: 10 MINUTES / COOK TIME: 25 MINUTES

The way to any Italian-American's heart is through a plate of inauthentic but totally delicious chicken Parmesan. Bake a batch of these crowd-pleasers as hors d'oeuvres and win over all your guests. Or serve for dinner with Rhode Island Red Marinara Sauce (page 221) and zucchini noodles.

1 pound free-range ground chicken

1 large free-range egg, lightly beaten

1 cup freshly grated organic Parmesan cheese

¾ cup shredded organic mozzarella cheese

¼ cup organic cream cheese, at room temperature

2 tablespoons water

3 garlic cloves, minced

1 teaspoon onion powder

½ teaspoon Italian seasoning

½ teaspoon sea salt

½ teaspoon freshly ground black pepper

8 slices organic provolone cheese, cut into strips

1. Preheat the oven to 450°F.

2. Line a baking pan with parchment paper.

3. In a large bowl, combine the chicken, egg, Parmesan and mozzarella cheeses, cream cheese, water, garlic, onion powder, Italian seasoning, salt, and pepper. Use your hands to mix the ingredients well.

4. Form the mixture into about 20 meatballs, placing them in the baking pan as you do.

5. Bake the meatballs until they reach an internal temperature of 165°F, about 18 minutes.

6. Remove the pan from the oven and turn the oven to broil.

7. Place the strips of provolone over the meatballs. Place them under the broiler until the cheese bubbles, 3 to 5 minutes. Serve hot.

PER SERVING: CALORIES: 508; TOTAL FAT: 31G; SATURATED FAT: 17G; PROTEIN: 53G; CHOLESTEROL: 182MG; CARBOHYDRATES: 3G; FIBER: 0G; **NET CARBS: 3G**

FAT: 55% / CARBS: 4% / PROTEIN: 41%

BLUE CHEESE BUFFALO CHICKEN BALLS

SERVES 4 TO 6 / PREP TIME: 10 MINUTES / COOK TIME: 18 MINUTES

1 pound free-range ground chicken

1 large free-range egg, lightly beaten

1 cup shredded organic mozzarella cheese

½ cup crumbled organic blue cheese

¼ cup chopped celery

2 tablespoons water

1 teaspoon onion powder

½ teaspoon sea salt

½ teaspoon freshly ground black pepper

1 recipe Buffalo Sauce (page 223)

For a quick snack or a party dish you can serve with fancy little toothpicks, these slightly spicy buffalo balls, packed with rich blue cheese, are just the ticket.

1. Preheat the oven to 450°F.
2. Line a baking pan with parchment paper.
3. In a large bowl, combine the chicken, egg, mozzarella and blue cheeses, celery, water, onion powder, salt, and pepper. Use your hands to mix the ingredients well.
4. Form the mixture into about 20 meatballs, placing them in the baking pan as you do.
5. Bake until the internal temperature reaches 165°F, about 18 minutes.
6. Meanwhile warm the buffalo sauce in a medium saucepan over low heat.
7. When the meatballs are done, toss them in the warm sauce and serve.

PER SERVING: CALORIES: 340; TOTAL FAT: 17G;
SATURATED FAT: 6G; PROTEIN: 44G; CHOLESTEROL: 157MG;
CARBOHYDRATES: 2G; FIBER: 0G; **NET CARBS: 2G**

FAT: 45% / CARBS: 3% / PROTEIN: 52%

BUTTERY GARLIC BOMB
CRISPY CHICKEN THIGHS

SERVES 2 / PREP TIME: 10 MINUTES / COOK TIME: 35 MINUTES

Crispy chicken skin tops these flavorful thighs that cook in a garlic, onion, thyme, and tarragon base. Definitely lip-smacking and finger-licking good.

4 bone-in, skin-on free-range chicken thighs

10 garlic cloves, peeled

1 white onion, quartered

¼ cup Golden Ghee (page 224), melted

1 teaspoon chopped fresh tarragon leaves

1 teaspoon fresh thyme leaves

Sea salt

Freshly ground black pepper

1 lemon

1. Preheat the oven to 450°F.

2. Place the chicken thighs in a cast iron or ovenproof skillet. Wedge the garlic cloves and onion quarters between the thighs. Drizzle the ghee over the chicken, then sprinkle with the tarragon, thyme, salt, and pepper. Last, squeeze the juice from the lemon over the top (use a strainer to catch any seeds).

3. Bake the chicken thighs until cooked through, about 30 minutes.

4. When the chicken is done, turn on the broiler and place the chicken under the broiler until the skin is crispy, about 5 minutes.

5. Serve with the roasted onion quarters and delicious roasted garlic.

PER SERVING: CALORIES: 743; TOTAL FAT: 64G; SATURATED FAT: 30G; PROTEIN: 35G; CHOLESTEROL: 262MG; CARBOHYDRATES: 9G; FIBER: 2G; **NET CARBS: 7G**

FAT: 77% / CARBS: 5% / PROTEIN: 18%

SIMPLE COCONUT-LEMONGRASS CHICKEN AND KALE

SERVES 2 / PREP TIME: 10 MINUTES / COOK TIME: 40 MINUTES

4 bone-in, skin-on free-range chicken thighs

5 garlic cloves, peeled

1 cup unsweetened coconut milk

¼ cup Golden Ghee (page 224)

½ teaspoon ground cinnamon

1 lemongrass stalk, chopped

1 lemon

Sea salt

Freshly ground black pepper

3 cups torn kale leaves

Chicken is complemented by a light coconut and lemongrass infusion, which is married to kale in the end.

1. Preheat the oven to 450°F.

2. Place the chicken thighs in a cast iron or ovenproof skillet. Wedge the garlic cloves between the thighs.

3. In a small microwave-safe bowl, combine the coconut milk, ghee, and cinnamon and microwave for 15 seconds to melt the ghee. Mix thoroughly.

4. Drizzle the sauce over the chicken, then add the lemongrass around and between the thighs. Squeeze the juice from the lemon over the top of the chicken (use a strainer to catch any seeds) and season generously with salt and pepper.

5. Bake the chicken until it is cooked through, about 30 minutes.

6. When the chicken is done, turn on the broiler and place the chicken under the broiler until the skin is crispy, about 5 minutes. Transfer the chicken and garlic to serving plates (discard the lemongrass).

7. Place the skillet on the stove over medium heat and add the kale. Wilt the kale, tossing frequently, about 5 minutes. Serve the kale with the chicken.

PER SERVING: CALORIES: 634; TOTAL FAT: 46G; SATURATED FAT: 23G; PROTEIN: 47G; CHOLESTEROL: 262MG; CARBOHYDRATES: 13G; FIBER: 4G; **NET CARBS: 9G**

FAT: 63% / CARBS: 8% / PROTEIN: 29%

CHILI-LIME DRUMSTICKS

SERVES 4 / PREP TIME: 5 MINUTES / COOK TIME: 40 MINUTES

Drumsticks are one of the least expensive meats, next to chicken thighs and pork cutlets. Here the drumsticks are coated in a spicy, sweet chili-lime dressing.

1. Preheat the oven to 400°F.

2. Line a rimmed baking sheet with parchment paper and place a wire rack on it.

3. In a bowl, toss the drumsticks with ¼ cup of marinade.

4. Place the drumsticks on the wire rack and bake until cooked through, about 40 minutes, basting them with the remaining ¼ cup of marinade halfway through.

24 free-range chicken drumsticks

½ cup Chili-Lime Marinade (page 228), divided

PER SERVING: CALORIES: 895; TOTAL FAT: 59G;
SATURATED FAT: 10G; PROTEIN: 78G; CHOLESTEROL: 243MG;
CARBOHYDRATES: 4G; FIBER: 0G; **NET CARBS: 4G**

FAT: 62% / CARBS: 2% / PROTEIN: 36%

SLOW COOKER LEMON-ROSEMARY CHICKEN

SERVES 2 TO 4 / PREP TIME: 10 MINUTES / COOK TIME: 6 TO 8 HOURS

1 whole free-range chicken

1 tablespoon Golden Ghee (page 224), melted

1 teaspoon sea salt

½ teaspoon freshly ground black pepper

1 lemon, quartered

1 tablespoon chopped fresh rosemary leaves

10 garlic cloves, peeled

Throw a few ingredients in your slow cooker in the morning, and come home to a fully cooked meal. When you're done with this chicken, use the bones for Lemon-Rosemary Bone Broth (page 193) and get several more meals out of it.

1. Place the chicken in the slow cooker. Rub it all over with the ghee and season it with the salt and pepper.

2. Squeeze the juice from 1 lemon quarter over the chicken and store the rind and a second lemon quarter inside the chicken cavity. Place the remaining two lemon quarters on top of the chicken legs.

3. Sprinkle the chicken with the rosemary and place the garlic cloves inside the chicken cavity.

4. Cover and cook for 6 to 8 hours on low. Serve hot.

PER SERVING: CALORIES: 693; TOTAL FAT: 37G;
SATURATED FAT: 15G; PROTEIN: 68G; CHOLESTEROL: 229MG;
CARBOHYDRATES: 6G; FIBER: 1G; **NET CARBS: 5G**

FAT: 48% / CARBS: 13% / PROTEIN: 39%

LEMON-ROSEMARY BONE BROTH

MAKES 2½ QUARTS / PREP TIME: 10 MINUTES / COOK TIME: 12 TO 24 HOURS

Use this savory bone broth in other recipes or sip it when you get a cold. The apple cider vinegar is a must; it helps extract the minerals and nutrients from the bones. If you can find it, try using pink Himalayan salt instead of sea salt. Pink Himalayan salt contains minerals like sulfate, magnesium, calcium, and potassium. Freeze in 1-cup containers until needed.

1. Combine the garlic cloves, celery, water, vinegar, bay leaves, onion powder, and salt in the slow cooker. Add the chicken carcass, cover, and cook for at least 12 hours on low or, preferably, up to 24 hours.

2. Skim off any excess fat from the top of the broth. Pour the broth through several layers of cheese-cloth or a fine-mesh strainer.

PER SERVING (1 CUP): CALORIES: 76; TOTAL FAT: 4G; SATURATED FAT: 1G; PROTEIN: 8G; CHOLESTEROL: 7MG; CARBOHYDRATES: 2G; FIBER: 0G; **NET CARBS: 2G**

FAT: 48% / CARBS: 10% / PROTEIN: 42%

Carcass from Slow Cooker Lemon-Rosemary Chicken (page 192), lemons discarded, garlic cloves reserved

3 celery stalks, including leaves

10 cups water

1 tablespoon apple cider vinegar

2 bay leaves

1 tablespoon onion powder

1 tablespoon sea salt

RECIPE TIP *You can make this broth with any chicken recipe. It makes a better broth if you cook the chicken in the slow cooker first, and then simply add the remaining ingredients once you've plucked the meat off for your dinner(s).*

CHAPTER TEN

DESSERTS

SUGAR-FREE VANILLA BEAN SWEETENER

MAKES ABOUT 1 CUP / PREP TIME: 5 MINUTES / COOK TIME: 10 MINUTES

1 cup water

½ cup erythritol

1 drop liquid stevia

2 teaspoons pure organic vanilla bean extract

1 vanilla bean pod, halved lengthwise and seeds scraped out

RECIPE TIP *If the sweetener solidifies a bit, throw it in the blender until smooth.*

In many of the recipes in this chapter, and a few in other chapters, you'll find that a little vanilla sweetener makes all the difference. You can buy your own low- to zero-carb vanilla syrup inexpensively; Torani (made with Splenda) and Monin (made with Splenda and erythritol) are popular. I included this recipe for a homemade version because, instead of asking you to keep a bag of erythritol and a jar of stevia on hand for dessert recipes that often require way too much of both, I've simplified all the recipes in this book so this one sweetener is all you'll need—and not a whole lot of it.

1. In a small saucepan, bring the water to a boil over high heat. Reduce the heat to low and add the erythritol, stevia, vanilla extract, and vanilla seeds.

2. Simmer the syrup, stirring frequently, until it has reduced by about half, about 10 minutes.

3. Pour the syrup into a jar with a tight-fitting lid; refrigerate for up to 2 weeks.

PER SERVING (1 TEASPOON): CALORIES: 0; TOTAL FAT: 0G; SATURATED FAT: 0G; PROTEIN: 0G; CHOLESTEROL: 0MG; CARBOHYDRATES: 2G; FIBER: 0G; **NET CARBS: 2G**

FAT: 0% / CARBS: 100% / PROTEIN: 0%

WHIPPED CREAM

SERVES 6 / PREP TIME: 20 SECONDS

If I didn't include this simple whipped cream recipe, you might not have known how easy and satisfying it is. Get yourself a single-serving blender and you'll make this in mere seconds.

In a single-serving blender, combine the heavy cream and sweetener (if using) and blend until the liquid stops moving because it has turned into fluffy whipped cream, 10 to 15 seconds. The whipped cream is best if used immediately, but it can be refrigerated in an airtight container for a day.

PER SERVING: CALORIES: 69; TOTAL FAT: 7G;
SATURATED FAT: 5G; PROTEIN: 0G; CHOLESTEROL: 27MG;
CARBOHYDRATES: 1G; FIBER: 0G; **NET CARBS: 1G**

FAT: 92% / CARBS: 8% / PROTEIN: 0%

1 cup organic heavy (whipping) cream

1 tablespoon Sugar-Free Vanilla Bean Sweetener (page 196; optional)

MIXED BERRY AND SAGE FRUIT SALAD

SERVES 1 / PREP TIME: 5 MINUTES

½ cup blackberries

½ cup raspberries

¼ cup sliced strawberries

1 tablespoon blueberries

1 large fresh sage
leaf, chopped

1 teaspoon freshly
squeezed Meyer
lemon juice

1 teaspoon Sugar-Free
Vanilla Bean Sweetener
(page 196; optional)

RECIPE TIP *The Meyer lemon
is a hybrid of a lemon and
a mandarin orange, making
it sweeter than a lemon, but
without the added sugars of
oranges. One Meyer lemon
has 4 to 5 net carbs.*

*Berries are the ultimate whole food keto dessert.
Blackberries, raspberries, strawberries, and
blueberries are low carb, with net carbs increasing
in that order, so fill up more on blackberries, less
on blueberries.*

In a small bowl, toss together all the ingredients
and serve.

PER SERVING: CALORIES: 81; TOTAL FAT: 1G;
SATURATED FAT: 0G; PROTEIN: 2G; CHOLESTEROL: 0MG;
CARBOHYDRATES: 18G; FIBER: 9G; **NET CARBS: 9G**

FAT: 10% / CARBS: 81% / PROTEIN: 9%

BLACKBERRY AND SAGE ICE POPS

SERVES 6 TO 8 / PREP TIME: 5 MINUTES

Traditional ice pops are just sugar and water. The ice-cream truck rolled up, and your parents were charged $3 for less than a cup of sugar and water, frozen onto a stick. You loved the heck out of that thing. Well, no more, I say. These ice pops may well cost a few bucks to make, but they're all fruit, baby. They are deliciously fresh and naturally sweet enough to enjoy as a frozen treat, and the added sage is a perfect complement.

In a blender, combine all the ingredients and blend until smooth. Pour into ice pop sleeves or molds. Freeze overnight.

PER SERVING: CALORIES: 10; TOTAL FAT: 0G; SATURATED FAT: 0G; PROTEIN: 0G; CHOLESTEROL: 0MG; CARBOHYDRATES: 2G; FIBER: 1G; **NET CARBS: 1G**

FAT: 0% / CARBS: 100% / PROTEIN: 0%

1 cup blackberries

2 fresh sage leaves

½ cup water

1 teaspoon Sugar-Free Vanilla Bean Sweetener (page 196; optional)

RECIPE TIP *Strawberry and sage is another wonderful combination, albeit a little less sweet than the blackberries.*

STRAWBERRY-LIME SORBET

SERVES 6 / PREP TIME: 5 MINUTES, PLUS FREEZING TIME

1 cup organic heavy (whipping) cream

3 cups chopped strawberries

Grated zest of 1 lime

3 tablespoons kosher gelatin

2 tablespoons Sugar-Free Vanilla Bean Sweetener (page 196)

I've always been a sorbet kind of gal. The creamy sweetness of a fruit-flavored frozen treat could beat out rocky road any day. It still does on keto, especially with a dose of sweet cream.

1. In a single-serving blender, blend the heavy cream, strawberries, lime zest, gelatin, and sweetener on high until the mixture is thick like whipped cream and no longer spins with the blades, 30 to 60 seconds.

2. Pour the mixture into an ice-cream maker and follow the manufacturer's instructions to freeze the sorbet, or pour it into a small container with a tight-fitting lid and freeze for at least 2 hours.

PER SERVING: CALORIES: 104; TOTAL FAT: 8G; SATURATED FAT: 5G; PROTEIN: 5G; CHOLESTEROL: 27MG; CARBOHYDRATES: 5G; FIBER: 1G; **NET CARBS: 4G**

FAT: 69% / CARBS: 17% / PROTEIN: 14%

MEYER LEMON CUSTARD

SERVES 2 / PREP TIME: 10 MINUTES / COOK TIME: 15 MINUTES, PLUS 3 HOURS TO CHILL

A good custard is key to any ketogenic dessert. Eggs and almond milk are cooked slowly to form a creamy custard, while sweet Meyer lemon and vanilla make it taste like spring.

1. In a single-serving blender, combine the eggs, almond milk, lemon juice, and sweetener and blend to mix thoroughly.

2. Transfer the mixture to a small saucepan and heat it over medium-low heat, stirring frequently, until thick, about 15 minutes.

3. Pour the custard into two 3½-inch ramekins. Sprinkle the lemon zest on top. Cover the ramekins with plastic wrap and refrigerate for at least 3 hours.

2 large free-range eggs

1 cup unsweetened almond milk

3 tablespoons freshly squeezed Meyer lemon juice

2 tablespoons Sugar-Free Vanilla Bean Sweetener (page 196)

1 teaspoon grated Meyer lemon zest

PER SERVING: CALORIES: 83; TOTAL FAT: 6G;
SATURATED FAT: 2G; PROTEIN: 6G; CHOLESTEROL: 164MG;
CARBOHYDRATES: 1G; FIBER: 1G; **NET CARBS: 0G**

FAT: 65% / CARBS: 0% / PROTEIN: 35%

LEMON CURD TARTS

SERVES 6 / PREP TIME: 20 MINUTES / COOK TIME: 20 MINUTES, PLUS OVERNIGHT TO CHILL

½ cup (1 stick) plus
3 tablespoons unsalted
grass-fed butter,
melted, divided

¾ cup almond meal

4 large free-range
egg yolks

Grated zest of 3 lemons

½ cup freshly squeezed
lemon juice

¼ cup Sugar-Free
Vanilla Bean Sweetener
(page 196)

Who'da thunk that lemon and eggs could make such a zesty, sweet treat? Heating the egg yolks pasteurizes them, making them safe to eat in these sweet, creamy tarts.

1. Line a 12-count mini-muffin tin with parchment cups.

2. In a small bowl, stir 3 tablespoons of melted butter into the almond meal. Press the crust into the bottoms of the mini-muffin cups.

3. In a blender or food processor, blend the egg yolks, lemon zest and juice, sweetener, and the remaining ½ cup of melted butter until smooth.

4. Transfer the filling to a small saucepan. Cook the filling over low heat, stirring constantly, until thick, about 15 minutes.

5. Pour the filling into the mini-muffin cups, cover the tin with plastic wrap, and refrigerate overnight.

PER SERVING: CALORIES: 296; TOTAL FAT: 30G;
SATURATED FAT: 15G; PROTEIN: 5G; CHOLESTEROL: 196MG;
CARBOHYDRATES: 3G; FIBER: 2G; **NET CARBS: 1G**

FAT: 91% / CARBS: 2% / PROTEIN: 7%

MASCARPONE CREAM CHEESE–FILLED STRAWBERRIES

SERVES 3 / PREP TIME: 15 MINUTES, PLUS 30 MINUTES TO CHILL

Cheesecake is never too far away with this super simple creamy filling piped into juicy, sweet strawberries, then topped with almond meal that impersonates a crumbly graham cracker crust quite well.

1. Put the almond meal on a plate or in a shallow bowl.

2. Hull the strawberries and use a small melon baller to scoop out some of the flesh from inside to allow each strawberry to be filled.

3. In a small microwave-safe bowl, microwave the cream cheese and mascarpone until melted. Stir to mix thoroughly, then stir in the sweetener.

4. Transfer the filling to a zipper-top plastic bag and cut off a small piece of one corner at the bottom. Pipe the filling into the strawberries. Gently press the top of each strawberry into the almond flour.

5. Place the strawberries in an airtight container and refrigerate for 30 minutes before serving.

¼ cup almond meal

10 small or 5 large strawberries

¼ cup organic cream cheese

2 tablespoons organic mascarpone

1 tablespoon Sugar-Free Vanilla Bean Sweetener (page 196)

PER SERVING: CALORIES: 138; TOTAL FAT: 13G;
SATURATED FAT: 5G; PROTEIN: 5G; CHOLESTEROL: 26MG;
CARBOHYDRATES: 4G; FIBER: 2G; **NET CARBS: 2G**

FAT: 80% / CARBS: 5% / PROTEIN: 15%

FROZEN BLACK FOREST PUDDING

SERVES 4 / PREP TIME: 10 MINUTES / COOK TIME: 20 MINUTES, PLUS CHILLING/FREEZING TIME

1 cup organic heavy (whipping) cream

1 cup unsweetened almond milk

3 cherries, pitted and chopped

½ cup unsweetened cocoa powder

Pinch sea salt

2 large free-range egg yolks

¼ cup Sugar-Free Vanilla Bean Sweetener (page 196)

Crunchy almonds complement this rich, chocolate frozen treat, which in itself is infused with sweet wild cherries. It can be made easily in a home ice-cream maker.

1. In a medium saucepan, heat the heavy cream, almond milk, cherries, cocoa powder, and salt over medium heat until hot, about 3 minutes. Remove the cherries with a slotted spoon and set them aside.

2. In a medium bowl, beat the egg yolks. While constantly whisking, slowly pour the hot cream mixture into the eggs. (It's important to pour slowly so the heat doesn't scramble the eggs.)

3. Pour the mixture back into the pot and cook, stirring constantly with a spatula to scrape the sides and bottom of the pot, until it is thick and coats the back of a spatula, about 15 minutes. Once it has thickened, stir in the sweetener.

4. Pour the mixture into an airtight container and refrigerate until cold, about 2 hours.

5. Transfer the mixture to an ice-cream maker and follow the manufacturer's instructions.

6. When the ice cream is ready, fold in the chopped cherries, then freeze in an airtight container until firm, about 3 hours.

PER SERVING: CALORIES: 166; TOTAL FAT: 16G; SATURATED FAT: 9G; PROTEIN: 4G; CHOLESTEROL: 146MG; CARBOHYDRATES: 8G; FIBER: 4G; **NET CARBS: 4G**

FAT: 88% / CARBS: 6% / PROTEIN: 6%

FROZEN PUMPKIN SPICE LATTE

SERVES 4 / PREP TIME: 5 MINUTES / COOK TIME: 20 MINUTES, PLUS CHILLING/FREEZING TIME

Infused with the flavors of autumn, this pumpkin spice latte begins with a creamy espresso base infused with spices such as cinnamon and cloves, and a kiss of orange zest.

1. In a medium saucepan, heat the pumpkin, heavy cream, espresso, and ground spices over medium heat until hot, about 3 minutes.

2. In a small bowl, beat the egg yolks. While constantly whisking, slowly pour the hot pumpkin mixture into the egg yolks. It's important to do this slowly to keep from scrambling the eggs.

3. Pour the mixture back into the pot and cook, stirring constantly with a spatula to scrape the sides and bottom of the pot, until it is thick and coats the back of a spatula, about 15 minutes. Once it has thickened, stir in the sweetener and orange zest.

4. Pour the mixture into an airtight container and refrigerate until cold, about 2 hours.

5. Transfer the mixture to an ice-cream maker and follow the manufacturer's instructions.

½ cup pure pumpkin purée (not pumpkin pie filling)

½ cup organic heavy (whipping) cream

2 tablespoons cold espresso

½ teaspoon ground cinnamon

¼ teaspoon ground nutmeg

¼ teaspoon ground ginger

¼ teaspoon ground allspice

⅛ teaspoon ground cloves

2 large free-range egg yolks

3 tablespoons Sugar-Free Vanilla Bean Sweetener (page 196)

1 tablespoon grated orange zest

PER SERVING: CALORIES: 93; TOTAL FAT: 8G;
SATURATED FAT: 4G; PROTEIN: 2G; CHOLESTEROL: 125MG;
CARBOHYDRATES: 4G; FIBER: 1G; **NET CARBS: 3G**

FAT: 77% / CARBS: 13% / PROTEIN: 10%

RICOTTA-ALMOND DOUGHNUTS

SERVES 6 / PREP TIME: 10 MINUTES / COOK TIME: 12 MINUTES

Golden Ghee (page 224)

¼ cup organic
ricotta cheese

2 large free-range eggs

2 tablespoons
almond flour

1 tablespoon
coconut flour

1 teaspoon baking
powder

½ teaspoon ground
cinnamon

2 ounces unsweetened
chocolate

2 tablespoons unsalted
grass-fed butter

2 tablespoons Sugar-Free
Vanilla Bean Sweetener
(page 196)

Your preferred sweetener
to taste (optional)

It's true that deviled eggs, lobster, and ramen noodles hold a special place in my heart, but in my carb-binging days I loved doughnuts. I've driven days for doughnuts, woken up at dawn and waited hours in line for cronuts at Dominique Ansel Bakery, and once took a 3-hour "break" during a conference in California to drive to a place called Psycho Donuts near San Jose. My doughnut game is serious. With all that said, these mini doughnuts make an awesome dessert. Or breakfast/lunch/dinner.

1. Preheat the oven to 350°F.

2. Grease a 12-count mini-doughnut pan with ghee.

3. In a blender, blend the ricotta cheese, eggs, almond flour, coconut flour, baking powder, and cinnamon until smooth. Pour the batter into the doughnut cups, filling them two-thirds full.

4. Bake until a toothpick inserted in the center comes out clean, 10 to 12 minutes.

5. Remove the doughnuts from the tin and let them cool completely on a wire rack.

6. In a small microwave-safe bowl, combine the chocolate, butter, and sweeteners. Microwave on high in 15-second intervals, stirring after each one, until the chocolate is melted and the ingredients are thoroughly mixed.

7. Use a spoon to frost the cooled mini doughnuts.

PER SERVING: CALORIES: 144; TOTAL FAT: 14G;
SATURATED FAT: 7G; PROTEIN: 5G; CHOLESTEROL: 69MG;
CARBOHYDRATES: 3G; FIBER: 2G; **NET CARBS: 1G**

FAT: 85% / CARBS: 2% / PROTEIN: 13%

MAPLE-ORANGE SPICE MUG CAKE

SERVES 1 / PREP TIME: 10 MINUTES / COOK TIME: 2 MINUTES

One morning I was having breakfast in a cafe in Coeur d'Alene, Idaho, and I opted for the tea that the waitress raved about and said was "imported" from Seattle. One sip of this spicy cinnamon-orange bomb and I was hooked. Several hours later, I was in the MarketSpice tea shop in Seattle's Pike Place Market buying all the boxes I could find. I knew the flavors would be the perfect combination for a simple and wonderful mug cake that takes just a couple minutes to prepare but will keep your taste buds entertained long after. If you wish, sprinkle the mug cake with a little more cinnamon and/or top with a dollop of Whipped Cream (page 197).

1 large free-range egg

2 tablespoons Sugar-Free Vanilla Bean Sweetener (page 196)

½ teaspoon maple extract

½ teaspoon orange extract

2 tablespoons almond flour

½ teaspoon baking powder

⅛ teaspoon ground cinnamon

2 tablespoons Golden Ghee (page 224), melted but not hot

1. Crack the egg into a microwave-safe mug and use a fork to lightly beat it. Add the sweetener and maple and orange extracts, and stir to combine.

2. In a small bowl, mix the almond flour, baking powder, and cinnamon, then add the mixture to the mug and stir to blend.

3. Stir in the ghee.

4. Microwave the mug on high for 2 minutes.

5. The cake can be eaten right from the mug (let it cool for a moment first) or inverted onto a plate.

PER SERVING: CALORIES: 392; TOTAL FAT: 37G; SATURATED FAT: 18G; PROTEIN: 67G; CHOLESTEROL: 229MG; CARBOHYDRATES: 4G; FIBER: 2G; **NET CARBS: 2G**

FAT: 88% / CARBS: 3% / PROTEIN: 9%

NO-BAKE PUMPKIN PIE MUG CHEESECAKE

SERVES 1 / PREP TIME: 10 MINUTES, PLUS 3 HOURS TO CHILL

2 tablespoons
almond meal

4½ teaspoons unsalted
grass-fed butter, divided

¼ cup organic cream
cheese, at room
temperature

2 tablespoons organic
heavy (whipping) cream

2 tablespoons pure
pumpkin purée (not
pumpkin pie filling)

1 tablespoon Sugar-Free
Vanilla Bean Sweetener
(page 196)

⅛ teaspoon pumpkin
pie spice

Pinch nutmeg

Though this recipe serves one, you can make multiples for dinner parties where you need a keto-rific dessert idea. This creamy pumpkin cheesecake tastes like what would happen if spicy pumpkin pie and sweet cheesecake had a love affair.

1. In a microwave-safe mug, combine the almond meal and 1½ teaspoons of butter and microwave on high for 30 seconds. Stir the butter and almond meal together and use a spoon to flatten the mixture into the bottom of the mug to form a crust.

2. In a small bowl or single-serving blender, cream together the cream cheese, heavy cream, pumpkin, sweetener, pumpkin pie spice, and the remaining 3 teaspoons of butter.

3. Pour the mixture into the mug, sprinkle it with a little nutmeg, and refrigerate for 3 hours before serving.

PER SERVING: CALORIES: 475; TOTAL FAT: 49G;
SATURATED FAT: 27G; PROTEIN: 7G; CHOLESTEROL: 131MG;
CARBOHYDRATES: 5G; FIBER: 2G; **NET CARBS: 3G**

FAT: 92% / CARBS: 2% / PROTEIN: 6%

MINI COCONUT PIES

SERVES 12 / PREP TIME: 10 MINUTES, PLUS 30 MINUTES TO CHILL / COOK TIME: 10 MINUTES

Coconut is practically a food group when it comes to a whole food approach to the ketogenic lifestyle. So, consider this my contribution to the delicious bandwagon—a bite-size crispy coconut shell with a fluffy cream center.

1 tablespoon coconut oil

1 cup coconut flour

2 large free-range eggs

½ cup Golden Ghee (page 224), melted

3 tablespoons Sugar-Free Vanilla Bean Sweetener (page 196), divided

1 cup unsweetened coconut cream

¼ cup unsweetened shredded coconut

1. Preheat the oven to 350°F.

2. Grease the cups of a 12-count mini-muffin tin with coconut oil.

3. In a small bowl, whisk together the coconut flour, eggs, ghee, and 1 tablespoon of sweetener.

4. Divide the flour mixture between the mini-muffin cups and pat into the bottom of each cup.

5. Bake for 10 minutes. Allow to cool completely, then remove the little coconut pie shells from the tin.

6. In a small bowl, combine the coconut cream, shredded coconut, and the remaining 2 tablespoons of sweetener and mix thoroughly.

7. Top each pie shell with about 1 tablespoon of the cream mixture. Chill the pies for at least 30 minutes before serving.

PER SERVING: CALORIES: 174; TOTAL FAT: 13G;
SATURATED FAT: 9G; PROTEIN: 3G; CHOLESTEROL: 50MG;
CARBOHYDRATES: 7G; FIBER: 4G; **NET CARBS: 3G**

FAT: 74% / CARBS: 18% / PROTEIN: 8%

STRAWBERRIES AND CREAM CAKE

SERVES 1 / PREP TIME: 10 MINUTES / COOK TIME: 4 MINUTES

2 large free-range eggs

¼ cup Sugar-Free Vanilla Bean Sweetener (page 196)

2 tablespoons Golden Ghee (page 224), melted but not hot

2 tablespoons organic cream cheese, at room temperature

¼ cup almond flour

4 strawberries, hulled and cut into chunks

¼ cup Whipped Cream (page 197)

This sweet, creamy cake filled with hot, plump straw-berries brings me back to those mornings when I snagged the only two packets of strawberries and cream oatmeal in the box.

1. In a single-serving blender, blend the eggs, sweet-ener, ghee, and cream cheese until well mixed. Scrape the mixture into a small microwave-safe bowl or mug.

2. Stir in the almond flour, then stir in the strawberries.

3. Microwave the batter on high for 4 minutes. Let the cake cool for a minute, then top it with the whipped cream.

PER SERVING: CALORIES: 719; TOTAL FAT: 67G; SATURATED FAT: 31G; PROTEIN: 15G; CHOLESTEROL: 456MG; CARBOHYDRATES: 10G; FIBER: 4G; **NET CARBS: 6G**

FAT: 84% / CARBS: 5% / PROTEIN: 11%

PEPPERMINT FUDGE FAT BOMB

SERVES 10 / PREP TIME: 10 MINUTES, PLUS 30 MINUTES TO FREEZE

My grandmother always had a box of thin mints. I once buried a box as a "treasure" and made a map for my cousin to find it. He was not impressed. These melt-in-your-mouth peppermint patties hit the same delicious spot.

1. Line 10 cups of a 12-count mini-cupcake tin with parchment cups.

2. In a single-serving blender, combine the coconut oil, 2 tablespoons of sweetener, 1 tablespoon of heavy cream, and the mint extract. Blend until thick, about 30 seconds. Pour the mixture into the mini-cupcake cups, filling each half full. Place the tin in the freezer.

3. Meanwhile, combine the ghee and chocolate in a small microwave-safe bowl. Microwave on high in 15-second intervals, stirring after each, until the chocolate becomes soft and mixes easily with the ghee.

4. Stir in the remaining 1 tablespoon of sweetener and 1 tablespoon of heavy cream and mix until smooth.

5. Remove the cupcake tin from the freezer. Fill the rest of each cup with the chocolate mixture. Return the tin to the freezer to chill for at least 30 minutes. Store in an airtight container in the freezer or refrigerator.

⅓ cup coconut oil, melted

3 tablespoons Sugar-Free Vanilla Bean Sweetener (page 196), divided

2 tablespoons organic heavy (whipping) cream, divided

1 teaspoon mint extract

2 tablespoons Golden Ghee (page 224)

1 ounce unsweetened chocolate

PER SERVING: CALORIES: 117; TOTAL FAT: 12G; SATURATED FAT: 10G; PROTEIN: 0G; CHOLESTEROL: 11MG; CARBOHYDRATES: 1G; FIBER: 0G; **NET CARBS: 1G**

FAT: 94% / CARBS: 6% / PROTEIN: 0%

PEANUT BUTTER FUDGE FAT BOMB

SERVES 10 / PREP TIME: 10 MINUTES, PLUS 30 MINUTES TO FREEZE

¼ cup smooth
peanut butter

4 tablespoons Golden
Ghee (page 224), divided

1½ tablespoons
Sugar-Free Vanilla
Bean Sweetener
(page 196), divided

1 ounce unsweetened
chocolate

1 tablespoon organic
heavy (whipping) cream

The first low-carb recipe I ever made was a peanut butter cup. Since those days I've upped the fat in these babies with dollops of sweet buttery ghee.

1. Line 10 cups of a 12-count mini-cupcake tin with parchment cups.

2. In a small bowl, mix the peanut butter, 2 tablespoons of ghee, and ½ tablespoon of sweetener until smooth. (Microwave it in a microwave-safe bowl for 10 to 15 seconds if necessary to get it smooth.) Pour the mixture into the mini-cupcake cups, filling each half full. Place the tin in the freezer.

3. In another small microwave-safe bowl, combine the remaining 2 tablespoons of ghee and the chocolate. Microwave on high in 15-second intervals, stirring after each, until the chocolate becomes soft and mixes easily with the ghee.

4. Stir in the remaining 1 tablespoon of sweetener and the heavy cream and mix until smooth.

5. Remove the cupcake tin from the freezer. Fill the rest of each cup with the chocolate mixture. Return the tin to the freezer to chill for at least 30 minutes. Store in an airtight container in the freezer or refrigerator.

PER SERVING: CALORIES: 102; TOTAL FAT: 10G;
SATURATED FAT: 5G; PROTEIN: 2G; CHOLESTEROL: 15MG;
CARBOHYDRATES: 2G; FIBER: 1G; **NET CARBS: 1G**

FAT: 88% / CARBS: 4% / PROTEIN: 8%

PEANUT BUTTER—AVOCADO FAT BOMBS

SERVES 6 / PREP TIME: 10 MINUTES, PLUS 3 HOURS TO FREEZE

Peanut butter takes the cake, so to speak, in these bite-size fat bombs that deliver a triple dose of amino acids from the coconut oil, healthy fats from the avocado, and digestive benefits from the rich, buttery ghee.

1. Line a 12-count mini-cupcake tin with parchment cups.

2. In a blender, combine the coconut oil, ghee, heavy cream, peanut butter, avocado, and sweetener. Blend until smooth.

3. Pour the mixture into the cupcake cups and freeze for at least 3 hours before serving.

½ cup coconut oil, melted

½ cup Golden Ghee (page 224), melted

3 tablespoons organic heavy (whipping) cream

1 cup peanut butter, smooth or chunky

1 avocado, peeled, pitted, and chopped

1 tablespoon Sugar-Free Vanilla Bean Sweetener (page 196)

PER SERVING: CALORIES: 653; TOTAL FAT: 68G; SATURATED FAT: 34G; PROTEIN: 12G; CHOLESTEROL: 54MG; CARBOHYDRATES: 9G; FIBER: 5G; **NET CARBS: 4G**

FAT: 92% / CARBS: 2% / PROTEIN: 6%

CHAPTER ELEVEN

RUBS, CONDIMENTS & SAUCES

SEASONED SALT

MAKES ABOUT ½ CUP / PREP TIME: 5 MINUTES

2 tablespoons sea salt

2 tablespoons
onion powder

1 tablespoon
sweet paprika

1 tablespoon chili powder

1 tablespoon
ground cumin

1 tablespoon ground
coriander

1 tablespoon dried parsley

1 tablespoon garlic salt

Season dishes from eggs Benedict to pork chops to ribeyes with this seasoned salt that blends the flavors of chili and cumin with sweet paprika and garlic.

Combine all the ingredients in an airtight container and give it a few shakes.

PER SERVING (1 TEASPOON): CALORIES: 5; TOTAL FAT: 0G; SATURATED FAT: 0G; PROTEIN: 0G; CHOLESTEROL: 0MG; CARBOHYDRATES: 1G; FIBER: 0G; **NET CARBS: 1G**

FAT: 0% / CARBS: 100% / PROTEIN: 0%

GOLDEN TACO SEASONING

MAKES ABOUT 1⅓ CUPS / PREP TIME: 10 MINUTES

A single packet of store-bought taco seasoning can store up to 20 net carbs of sugar and fillers. So, I started making my own. The turmeric adds a golden hue and warm, peppery notes to the blend—and is also considered an anti-inflammatory agent in Indian and Chinese medicine. Use 2 tablespoons of rub for every 1 pound of ground beef when making tacos.

Combine all the ingredients in an airtight container and give it a few shakes.

PER SERVING (1 TABLESPOON): CALORIES: 19; TOTAL FAT: 1G; SATURATED FAT: 0G; PROTEIN: 1G; CHOLESTEROL: 0MG; CARBOHYDRATES: 4G; FIBER: 2G; **NET CARBS: 2G**

FAT: 31% / CARBS: 55% / PROTEIN: 14%

6 tablespoons
chili powder

3 tablespoons
smoked paprika

3 tablespoons
ground cumin

3 tablespoons sea salt

3 tablespoons freshly
ground black pepper

1½ tablespoons
garlic powder

1½ tablespoons
onion powder

1 tablespoon
ground turmeric

EVERYDAY MEAT RUB

MAKES ABOUT 1 CUP / PREP TIME: 10 MINUTES

3 tablespoons paprika

3 tablespoons onion powder

3 tablespoons garlic powder

3 tablespoons sea salt

2 tablespoons chili powder

1 tablespoon dry brown mustard

1 tablespoon ground cumin

Ready to spice up your meats? This dry rub is great with any meat—grass-fed or organic, or course.

Combine all the ingredients in an airtight container and give it a few shakes.

PER SERVING (1 TABLESPOON): CALORIES: 17; TOTAL FAT: 1G; SATURATED FAT: 0G; PROTEIN: 1G; CHOLESTEROL: 0MG; CARBOHYDRATES: 3G; FIBER: 1G; **NET CARBS: 2G**

FAT: 53% / CARBS: 46% / PROTEIN: 1%

TANGY RANCH RUB

MAKES ABOUT 2 CUPS / PREP TIME: 10 MINUTES

This ranch rub can be used on beef, poultry, or pork. The buttermilk is the key ingredient, giving it that familiar ranch tang. Use 1 tablespoon of rub for every 1 pound of beef.

Combine all the ingredients in an airtight container and give it a few shakes.

PER SERVING (1 TEASPOON): CALORIES: 5; TOTAL FAT: 0G; SATURATED FAT: 0G; PROTEIN: 0G; CHOLESTEROL: 0MG; CARBOHYDRATES: 1G; FIBER: 0G; **NET CARBS: 1G**

FAT: 0% / CARBS: 100% / PROTEIN: 0%

6 tablespoons plus 2 teaspoons onion powder

6 tablespoons dried parsley

4 tablespoons dried oregano

4 tablespoons garlic salt

4 tablespoons sweet cream buttermilk powder

2 tablespoons dried dill weed

2 tablespoons garlic powder

2 tablespoons freshly ground black pepper

4 teaspoons dried basil

1 teaspoon dried thyme

1 teaspoon celery salt

HOMEMADE CHAMPAGNE KETCHUP

MAKES ABOUT 1½ CUPS / PREP TIME: 20 MINUTES / COOK TIME: 15 MINUTES

1 tablespoon extra-virgin olive oil

1 small yellow onion, chopped

1 cup tomato purée

¼ cup champagne vinegar

2 tablespoons water

1 tablespoon Sugar-Free Vanilla Bean Sweetener (page 196)

2 garlic cloves, minced

⅛ teaspoon ground cinnamon

⅛ teaspoon ground cardamom

⅛ teaspoon ground cloves

⅛ teaspoon ground star anise

⅛ teaspoon celery salt

⅛ teaspoon freshly ground black pepper

COOKING TIP *Depending on the tomato purée you buy, your ketchup may turn out too thick for your liking. Add 1 teaspoon of water at a time to the blender until it reaches your desired consistency.*

People are made from sugar, spice, and everything nice (wait, maybe that's dogs?). Likewise, ketchup is based on three primary ingredients: tomatoes, vinegar, and sugar. This ketogenic ketchup recipe is naturally sweetened by swapping out the typical onion powder for onion that has been browned to draw out its natural sweetness, then adding champagne vinegar. (You can use any vinegar, really, but champagne vinegar is sweeter.) Whip up a batch of this ketchup to serve with bunless hamburgers and stews.

1. In a medium saucepan, heat the olive oil over low heat, then brown the onion until it begins to soften, about 5 minutes.

2. Add the tomato purée, vinegar, water, sweetener, garlic, cinnamon, cardamom, cloves, star anise, celery salt, and pepper and bring everything to a simmer. Simmer the ketchup for 10 minutes.

3. Remove the pan from the heat and let the ketchup cool for 20 minutes. Pour the ketchup into a blender and blend until smooth.

4. Refrigerate the ketchup in an airtight container for up to 1 month.

PER SERVING (1 TABLESPOON): CALORIES: 13; TOTAL FAT: 1G; SATURATED FAT: 0G; PROTEIN: 0G; CHOLESTEROL: 0MG; CARBOHYDRATES: 1G; FIBER: 0G; **NET CARBS: 1G**

FAT: 70% / CARBS: 30% / PROTEIN: 0%

RHODE ISLAND RED MARINARA SAUCE

MAKES ABOUT 8 CUPS / PREP TIME: 10 MINUTES / COOK TIME: 40 MINUTES

When I kick the bucket, I want my grandkids to think, "There's nothing like Grandma's sauce!" My ultimate goal was a recipe that would have a slight spicy kick, since it couldn't be sweet, and that would use fresh tomatoes, nothing from a can. If I could do this, the world would be my oyster. In the process, I consulted a few chefs and a few grandmas. To my surprise, almost all use canned tomatoes, and some of them (gasp!) secretly use prepared tomato sauce in their mix. I decided to defy the odds and spent a whole winter making the perfect sauce using fresh tomatoes. The result is a blend of three plum tomatoes that have their own unique strengths in consistency, sweetness, and tartness. By making your own tomato paste, you'll bring out the sweetness of the tomatoes as they cara-melize in the oven.

1. Preheat the oven to 350°F.

2. Put the tomatoes in a blender or food processor and pulse several times until smooth (or still a bit chunky if you prefer your sauce that way).

3. In a medium saucepan, heat the olive oil over medium heat. When it is hot, add the onion and garlic and cook until soft, about 3 minutes.

4. Add the tomatoes, red wine, basil, onion powder, oregano, red pepper flakes, salt, and black pepper, and bring everything to a simmer. Reduce the heat to low.

»

12 ounces Roma tomatoes, diced

12 ounces Amish Paste tomatoes, diced

8 ounces San Marzano tomatoes, diced

2 tablespoons extra-virgin olive oil

½ sweet white onion, diced

3 garlic cloves, minced

2 tablespoons dry red wine

3 fresh basil leaves, chopped

1 teaspoon onion powder

1 teaspoon dried oregano

⅛ teaspoon red pepper flakes

Sea salt

Freshly ground black pepper

RECIPE TIP *If you can't find some of these tomato varieties, mix up 2 pounds of tomatoes. Plum tomatoes work best because they have less juice and reduce faster than larger tomatoes such as beefsteak.*

5. Transfer 2 cups of the sauce to an 8-by-8-inch baking dish. Continue to simmer the sauce in the pot for about 30 minutes. At the same time, put the baking dish with sauce in the oven and bake, stirring every 10 minutes so it doesn't burn, until the sauce becomes thick like a tomato paste, about 30 minutes.

6. Stir the paste into the tomato sauce and let it simmer a little longer, about 5 minutes.

7. Use an immersion blender (or pour the sauce into a standing blender) to blend the sauce one more time. This is an important step to get the most flavor and consistency from the fresh tomatoes, especially if you're not using the sauce right away.

PER SERVING (½ CUP): CALORIES: 30; TOTAL FAT: 2G; SATURATED FAT: 0G; PROTEIN: 1G; CHOLESTEROL: 0MG; CARBOHYDRATES: 3G; FIBER: 1G; **NET CARBS: 2G**

FAT: 60% / CARBS: 27% / PROTEIN: 13%

BUFFALO SAUCE

MAKES ABOUT 2 CUPS / PREP TIME: 5 MINUTES / COOK TIME: 10 MINUTES

I like to think that my years of Buffalo wing tasting and analysis resulted in a standout recipe that sports and pub fans alike will enjoy.

In a small saucepan, melt the butter over low heat. Once melted, add the hot sauce, garlic, paprika, salt, black pepper, and cayenne pepper and cook for 5 minutes. Store in an airtight container in the refrigerator for up to 1 week.

———

PER SERVING (2 TABLESPOONS): CALORIES: 105; TOTAL FAT: 11G; SATURATED FAT: 7G; PROTEIN: 0G; CHOLESTEROL: 31MG; CARBOHYDRATES: 1G; FIBER: 0G; **NET CARBS: 1G**

FAT: 96% / CARBS: 4% / PROTEIN: 0%

1 cup (2 sticks) salted grass-fed butter

1 cup hot sauce

4 garlic cloves, minced

1 teaspoon paprika

1 teaspoon sea salt

1 teaspoon freshly ground black pepper

½ teaspoon cayenne pepper

GOLDEN GHEE

MAKES ABOUT 1½ CUPS / PREP TIME: 5 MINUTES / COOK TIME: 15 MINUTES

2 cups (4 sticks)
unsalted grass-fed butter
such as Kerrygold

Imagine that your cooking oil tastes like butter. That's basically the concept of ghee. Pure, unsalted grass-fed butter is melted to a point where the milk solids, such as casein and lactose, can be removed, leaving a golden oil that can be cooked up to 500°F without burning. Ghee is highly regarded in India, where it is used to cook with but also consumed by the spoonful to aid in digestion. It also has a delightful balance of omega fatty acids.

1. Cut each butter stick into 10 cubes.

2. In a medium saucepan, heat the butter over medium-low heat until the butter separates and the milk solids fall to the bottom, 10 to 15 minutes. If you want a slightly nutty and rich browned-butter flavor, let the milk solids brown just slightly. Otherwise, remove the saucepan from the heat and skim off any foam from the top of the butter.

3. Strain the butter into a jar through several layers of cheesecloth or a fine-mesh strainer to remove all the solids.

4. Cover the jar and store at room temperature for up to 3 weeks or in the refrigerator for up to 3 months.

PER SERVING (1 TABLESPOON): CALORIES: 102; TOTAL FAT: 12G;
SATURATED FAT: 7G; PROTEIN: 0G; CHOLESTEROL: 30MG;
CARBOHYDRATES: 0G; FIBER: 0G; **NET CARBS: 0G**

FAT: 100% / CARBS: 0% / PROTEIN: 0%

ROASTED GARLIC AND SHALLOT BUTTER

MAKES ABOUT 1½ CUPS / PREP TIME: 10 MINUTES / COOK TIME: 30 MINUTES

This garlicky butter is delicious over green veggies such as asparagus and green beans. It's also a delicious topper for a thick ribeye steak.

1. Preheat the oven to 400°F.

2. Cut off the top (non-root end) of the garlic head, exposing most of the cloves.

3. Drizzle the olive oil over the top of the garlic. Wrap the head loosely in aluminum foil and place it in a small baking dish in case any oil escapes. Roast until the cloves are soft, about 30 minutes.

4. Meanwhile, in a medium saucepan, melt the ghee over medium heat. When it is hot, add the shallot and cook until soft, about 3 minutes. Using a slotted spoon, transfer the shallot onto a paper towel and pat dry.

5. Use a fork to transfer the roasted garlic cloves to a small bowl. Mash them into a paste. Add the shallot and butter and mix thoroughly, using an immersion blender if you prefer.

6. Refrigerate in an airtight container.

1 large head garlic

1 teaspoon extra-virgin olive oil

¼ cup Golden Ghee (page 224)

½ cup minced shallot

1 cup (2 sticks) salted grass-fed butter, at room temperature

---

PER SERVING (1 TABLESPOON): CALORIES: 97; TOTAL FAT: 10G; SATURATED FAT: 6G; PROTEIN: 0G; CHOLESTEROL: 26MG; CARBOHYDRATES: 2G; FIBER: 0G; **NET CARBS: 2G**

FAT: 93% / CARBS: 7% / PROTEIN: 0%

LEMON-DILL TARTAR SAUCE

MAKES ABOUT 1½ CUPS / PREP TIME: 10 MINUTES

1 cup mayonnaise

2 dill pickles, finely diced

1 tablespoon dill pickle juice

½ teaspoon freshly squeezed lemon juice

½ teaspoon onion powder

Pinch sea salt

Pinch freshly ground black pepper

When you're digging into your Lemon Parmesan–Crusted Fish Sticks (page 109) like a kid off the school bus, try this tangy sauce. It goes great with most other fish, too.

In a small bowl, combine all the ingredients. If not using right away, refrigerate in an airtight container for up to 3 days.

PER SERVING (2 TABLESPOONS): CALORIES: 85; TOTAL FAT: 9G; SATURATED FAT: 1G; PROTEIN: 0G; CHOLESTEROL: 5MG; CARBOHYDRATES: 1G; FIBER: 0G; **NET CARBS: 1G**

FAT: 95% / CARBS: 5% / PROTEIN: 0%

ITALIAN DRESSING

MAKES ABOUT 1½ CUPS / PREP TIME: 5 MINUTES

True Italian dressing is heavy on the oil, light on the vinegar, and salted just to taste. The dressing I grew up with was all of the above, plus some garlic. I've come to love the addition of basil, oregano, and marjoram in my dressing, too. The optional Romano cheese will add more depth of flavor.

1. In a blender, combine the olive oil, vinegar, basil, oregano, salt, pepper, and marjoram, and pulse for a few seconds to emulsify the oil. Stir in the garlic and cheese (if using).

2. For the best results, let the dressing rest overnight in an airtight jar to allow the flavors to develop and meld. The dressing can be refrigerated for up to 2 weeks.

3. If the oil solidifies, simply run the jar under warm water, or leave it out for an hour before serving.

1 cup high-quality extra-virgin olive oil

½ cup white vinegar

1 teaspoon dried basil

½ teaspoon dried oregano

¼ teaspoon sea salt

¼ teaspoon freshly ground black pepper

⅛ teaspoon dried marjoram

1 tablespoon minced garlic

2 tablespoons grated organic Pecorino Romano cheese (optional)

PER SERVING (2 TABLESPOONS): CALORIES: 147; TOTAL FAT: 17G; SATURATED FAT: 2G; PROTEIN: 0G; CHOLESTEROL: 0MG; CARBOHYDRATES: 0G; FIBER: 0G; **NET CARBS: 0G**

FAT: 100% / CARBS: 0% / PROTEIN: 0%

CHILI-LIME MARINADE

MAKES ABOUT ½ CUP / PREP TIME: 5 MINUTES

3 tablespoons extra-virgin olive oil

Juice of 3 limes

1½ tablespoons minced garlic

1½ teaspoons chili powder

1 teaspoon sea salt

½ teaspoon paprika

¼ teaspoon cayenne pepper

If I were a piece of chicken or steak, I'd want this marinade to make me the tastiest beast on the block. The marinade, which can also be used as a dressing, is slightly spicy but balanced by the lime.

Combine all the ingredients in an airtight jar and shake vigorously to blend. Keep refrigerated for up to 3 days.

PER SERVING (2 TABLESPOONS): CALORIES: 107; TOTAL FAT: 11G; SATURATED FAT: 2G; PROTEIN: 1G; CHOLESTEROL: 0MG; CARBOHYDRATES: 5G; FIBER: 1G; **NET CARBS: 4G**

FAT: 91% / CARBS: 8% / PROTEIN: 1%

GARLICKY MARINADE

MAKES ABOUT ¾ CUP / PREP TIME: 5 MINUTES

This light garlicky-herb drizzle is perfect for a big, fat mozzarella ball with sweet summer tomatoes. It goes just as well over steak. Use the highest-quality extra-virgin olive oil you can find.

Combine all the ingredients in an airtight jar and shake vigorously until thoroughly mixed.

PER SERVING (2 TABLESPOONS): CALORIES: 156; TOTAL FAT: 16G; SATURATED FAT: 3G; PROTEIN: 0G; CHOLESTEROL: 2MG; CARBOHYDRATES: 1G; FIBER: 0G; **NET CARBS: 1G**

FAT: 98% / CARBS: 2% / PROTEIN: 0%

½ cup high-quality extra-virgin olive oil

6 Perfect Roasted Garlic cloves (page 89), mashed

2 tablespoons chopped fresh basil

1 tablespoon Italian Dressing (page 227)

1 teaspoon sea salt

⅛ teaspoon red pepper flakes

AVOCADO-MINT SAUCE

MAKES ABOUT 1 CUP / PREP TIME: 5 MINUTES

1 avocado, peeled, pitted, and chopped

¼ cup organic heavy (whipping) cream

1 teaspoon freshly squeezed lime juice

1 fresh mint leaf

Pinch sea salt

KETO TIP *Replace the mint with 1 teaspoon chopped fresh cilantro and add ⅛ teaspoon garlic powder and ⅛ teaspoon onion powder to make a cream that complements Mexican-inspired dishes.*

This sauce is high in healthy fats and goes great over any lamb dish. Laced with cilantro, onion, and garlic, it also works well with cumin-flavored dishes like keto tacos.

In a single-serving blender or mini food processor, or in a bowl using an immersion blender, blend the avocado, heavy cream, lime juice, mint, and salt until mixed thoroughly.

PER SERVING (2 TABLESPOONS): CALORIES: 66; TOTAL FAT: 6G; SATURATED FAT: 2G; PROTEIN: 1G; CHOLESTEROL: 5MG; CARBOHYDRATES: 3G; FIBER: 2G; **NET CARBS: 1G**

FAT: 82% / CARBS: 9% / PROTEIN: 9%

ROASTED GARLIC CREAM

MAKES ABOUT 1 CUP / PREP TIME: 10 MINUTES / COOK TIME: 45 MINUTES

Garlic cream sauce can be dolloped on top of vegetables or steak—or eaten by the spoonful.

1. In a small saucepan, warm the olive oil over medium heat until it begins to shimmer. Add the garlic and salt, and reduce the heat to low. Cover and cook for 45 minutes.

2. Remove the pan from the heat and let cool to room temperature. Then pour the oil and garlic into a blender and blend until smooth. Refrigerate in an airtight container for up to 5 days.

PER SERVING (1 TABLESPOON): CALORIES: 30; TOTAL FAT: 3G; SATURATED FAT: 0G; PROTEIN: 0G; CHOLESTEROL: 0MG; CARBOHYDRATES: 1G; FIBER: 0G; **NET CARBS: 1G**

FAT: 90% / CARBS: 10% / PROTEIN: 0%

½ cup extra-virgin olive oil

20 garlic cloves, peeled

1 teaspoon sea salt

ROASTED GARLIC AND WALNUT PESTO

MAKES ABOUT 2 CUPS / PREP TIME: 10 MINUTES

4 cups fresh basil leaves

½ cup walnuts

2 tablespoons Roasted Garlic Cream (page 231)

1 teaspoon freshly squeezed lemon juice

1 teaspoon sea salt

1 cup grated organic Parmesan cheese

1½ cups extra-virgin olive oil

Walnuts have considerably fewer carbs than pine nuts (11 versus 18 per cup) and they add a welcome nuttiness to this roasted garlic–infused pesto.

In a food processor, pulse the basil, walnuts, garlic cream, lemon juice, and salt to break down the basil leaves. Add the Parmesan cheese and pulse to combine. Add the olive oil and pulse to combine. Refrigerate in an airtight container for up to 1 week.

PER SERVING (2 TABLESPOONS): CALORIES: 210; TOTAL FAT: 23G; SATURATED FAT: 4G; PROTEIN: 3G; CHOLESTEROL: 5MG; CARBOHYDRATES: 1G; FIBER: 0G; **NET CARBS: 1G**

FAT: 94% / CARBS: 2% / PROTEIN: 4%

BACON-MUSTARD GLAZE

MAKES ABOUT 1½ CUPS / PREP TIME: 10 MINUTES / COOK TIME: 15 MINUTES

Spicy mustard and smoky bacon dance across your taste buds with a surprise somersault in the middle when paired with pork chops or chicken.

1. In a skillet, crisp the bacon over medium heat, about 5 minutes.

2. Add the ghee. When it is melted, add the shallot and cook until soft and translucent, about 5 minutes.

3. Stir in the broth, Dijon mustard, creole mustard, and thyme. Bring to a boil, then reduce the heat to a simmer. Stir in the mascarpone, allowing it to melt and thicken the glaze, about 2 minutes. Use immediately.

PER SERVING (2 TABLESPOONS): CALORIES: 80; TOTAL FAT: 7G; SATURATED FAT: 3G; PROTEIN: 5G; CHOLESTEROL: 20MG; CARBOHYDRATES: 1G; FIBER: 1G; **NET CARBS: 0G**

FAT: 79% / CARBS: 0% / PROTEIN: 21%

1 pound uncured center-cut bacon, diced

2 tablespoons Golden Ghee (page 224)

1 shallot, diced

½ cup Lemon-Rosemary Bone Broth (page 193) or organic chicken broth

½ cup Dijon mustard

1 tablespoon creole mustard

1 tablespoon fresh thyme leaves

¼ cup organic mascarpone

SIMPLE GUACAMOLE

SERVES 10 / PREP TIME: 10 MINUTES

2 avocados, peeled,
pitted, and chopped

¼ cup chopped
fresh cilantro

¼ cup diced white onion

1 sweet tomato,
seeded and chopped

1 tablespoon freshly
squeezed lime juice

1 teaspoon minced garlic

¼ teaspoon sea salt

This recipe has all your favorites—creamy avocado, bright lime, and juicy tomato. It's the hit of every party.

In a small bowl, combine all the ingredients and mash together. Season with additional lime juice or salt as needed. Cover with plastic wrap and chill for 30 minutes before serving.

———————

PER SERVING: CALORIES: 86; TOTAL FAT: 8G;
SATURATED FAT: 2G; PROTEIN: 1G; CHOLESTEROL: 0MG;
CARBOHYDRATES: 4G; FIBER: 3G; **NET CARBS: 1G**

FAT: 84% / CARBS: 11% / PROTEIN: 5%

ROASTED RED PEPPERS

SERVES 10 / PREP TIME: 10 MINUTES / COOK TIME: 35 MINUTES

Roasted red peppers come in handy for a variety of recipes. There are about 4 net carbs in 1 cup of red peppers, so you can add a touch of their caramelized sweetness in any dish you like.

1. Preheat the oven to 450°F.
2. Line a rimmed baking sheet with aluminum foil.
3. Cut each red bell pepper in half and place the halves, skin-side up, on the baking sheet.
4. Drizzle the peppers all over with olive oil, then sprinkle with the garlic, oregano, salt, and pepper.
5. Bake the peppers until the skins char, 30 to 40 minutes.
6. Remove the peppers from the oven and let cool. Remove and discard the charred skins. Refrigerate the peppers in an airtight container for up to 1 week.

4 medium red bell peppers, tops and bottoms cut off, seeds and membranes removed

Extra-virgin olive oil

1 tablespoon minced garlic

Dried oregano

Sea salt

Freshly ground black pepper

PER SERVING: CALORIES: 40; TOTAL FAT: 3G;
SATURATED FAT: 0G; PROTEIN: 1G; CHOLESTEROL: 0MG;
CARBOHYDRATES: 3G; FIBER: 1G; **NET CARBS: 2G**

FAT: 70% / CARBS: 20% / PROTEIN: 10%

Acknowledgments

I'd like to thank every chef who has left a flavor on my tongue that I couldn't get out of my head. I recall a creamy crab claw dish in the French Quarter of New Orleans that blossomed my love for Cajun spices, and a cacciatore at a bar in Calistoga, California, that drove me to experiment with smoking peppers for tomato sauce. Thank you to every ketogenic and nonketogenic guest who gave me exactly the reaction I hoped for when they tasted one of my new dishes. A huge thanks to my husband, who has been my favorite taste tester and supporter of all. And to all the editors, nutritionists, and designers who have brought this cookbook to life, thank you for helping me introduce wholesome recipes to those who have embarked on a ketogenic journey.

APPENDIX A
A 4-Week Meal Plan

This meal plan is for your first month on the ketogenic diet. With the ultimate goal of staying within the 20 net carb range, I've included many of this book's recipes.

You'll find a net carb count for each recipe, a daily total, and a snack allowance. Snacks can vary from those in this book to macadamia nuts, cheeses, charcuterie, or smoothies. You may also put the snack allowance toward extra salads and sides to beef up meals.

Monday		Net Carbs
Breakfast	The Best Fried Eggs You'll Ever Eat (page 36)	2
Lunch	Lemon-Dill Tuna Salad (page 111)	2
Dinner	Buttery Garlic Bomb Crispy Chicken Thighs (page 189)	7

Snack Allowance (based on 20 net carbs per day) **9** / *Total Daily Net Carbs* **11**

Tuesday		Net Carbs
Breakfast	Garlic and Thyme Baked Egg (page 35)	1
Lunch	Mozzarella Crust Pizza (page 73)	3
Dinner	Lemon Cream Zoodles with Sweet Maine Lobster (page 116)	5

Snack Allowance (based on 20 net carbs per day) **11** / *Total Daily Net Carbs* **9**

Wednesday		Net Carbs
Breakfast	Mexican Chocolate Smoothie (page 61)	2
Lunch	Crisp Bacon and Blue Cheese Zoodles (page 95)	5
Dinner	Chicken topped with Creamed Spinach, Artichokes, and Red Pepper (page 91)	4

Snack Allowance (based on 20 net carbs per day) **9** / *Total Daily Net Carbs* **11**

Thursday

		Net Carbs
Breakfast	Toasted Cinnamon-Vanilla-Coconut Cereal (page 30)	3
Lunch	Spicy Lobster Salad (page 117)	2
Dinner	Baked Haddock, Sausage, and Sage (page 104)	7

Snack Allowance (based on 20 net carbs per day) **8** / *Total Daily Net Carbs* **12**

Friday

		Net Carbs
Breakfast	Scrambled Cinnamon and Cream Cheese Eggs (page 40)	1
Lunch	Pulled Buffalo Chicken Salad with Blue Cheese (page 173)	5
Dinner	Cajun Crab and Spaghetti Squash (page 113)	8

Snack Allowance (based on 20 net carbs per day) **6** / *Total Daily Net Carbs* **14**

Saturday

		Net Carbs
Breakfast	Lemon-Lavender Ricotta Pancakes (page 33)	2
Lunch	Dijon Steak and Cheese-Stuffed Peppers (page 143)	6
Dinner	Garlic-Thyme Beef Fondue (page 126)	4

Snack Allowance (based on 20 net carbs per day) **8** / *Total Daily Net Carbs* **12**

Sunday

		Net Carbs
Breakfast	Harvest Omelet (page 41)	3
Lunch	Veggie Fried Beef (page 127)	3
Dinner	Chicken Parmesan and Zoodles (page 176)	6

Snack Allowance (based on 20 net carbs per day) **8** / *Total Daily Net Carbs* **12**

Monday

		Net Carbs
Breakfast	Jerk Bacon (page 46) + eggs	0
Lunch	Salad of Brussels (page 85) + protein	5
Dinner	Tuscan Spinach and Havarti–Stuffed Pork Loin (page 169)	2

Snack Allowance (based on 20 net carbs per day) **13** / *Total Daily Net Carbs* **7**

Tuesday

		Net Carbs
Breakfast	Cinnamon Toast Pork Rinds (page 31)	0
Lunch	Ground beef with Golden Taco Seasoning (page 217) over lettuce	2
Dinner	Steak + Aglio e Olio Zoodles (page 96)	7

Snack Allowance (based on 20 net carbs per day) **11** / *Total Daily Net Carbs* **9**

Wednesday

		Net Carbs
Breakfast	Chocolate-Covered Strawberry Smoothie (page 59)	3
Lunch	White Anchovy and Lemon Arugula Salad (page 110)	4
Dinner	Roasted Pork Chops and Garlic Green Beans (page 166)	4

Snack Allowance (based on 20 net carbs per day) **9** / *Total Daily Net Carbs* **11**

Thursday

		Net Carbs
Breakfast	Garlic and Thyme Baked Egg (page 35)	1
Lunch	Cheese Bomb Italian Meatballs (page 129)	4
Dinner	Rosemary Pesto Cowboy Ribeye (page 136)	2

Snack Allowance (based on 20 net carbs per day) **13** / *Total Daily Net Carbs* **7**

Friday

		Net Carbs
Breakfast	Strawberries and Cream Cake (page 210)	6
Lunch	Sage Sausage Scotch Eggs (page 153)	2
Dinner	Bacon-Wrapped Tilapia (page 108)	2

Snack Allowance (based on 20 net carbs per day) **10** */ Total Daily Net Carbs* **10**

Saturday

		Net Carbs
Breakfast	Omelet with Asparagus and Spring Onions (page 43)	3
Lunch	Bacon-Ranch Quesadilla with Chicken (page 159)	2
Dinner	Three-Cheese Chicken Cordon Bleu (page 180) + Cauliflower Risotto (page 92)	8

Snack Allowance (based on 20 net carbs per day) **7** */ Total Daily Net Carbs* **13**

Sunday

		Net Carbs
Breakfast	Morning Meatloaf (page 47)	4
Lunch	Meatzza (page 130)	4
Dinner	Sausage and Kale Cream Soup (page 150)	3

Snack Allowance (based on 20 net carbs per day) **9** */ Total Daily Net Carbs* **11**

Monday

		Net Carbs
Breakfast	The Best Fried Eggs You'll Ever Eat (page 36)	2
Lunch	Burrata Caprese Salad (page 84)	3
Dinner	Walnut-Crusted Pork Chops (page 164)	1

Snack Allowance (based on 20 net carbs per day) **14** / *Total Daily Net Carbs* **6**

Tuesday

		Net Carbs
Breakfast	Toasted Cinnamon-Vanilla-Coconut Cereal (page 30)	3
Lunch	Lemon-Dill Tuna Salad (page 111)	2
Dinner	Five-Layer Mexican Casserole (page 132)	3

Snack Allowance (based on 20 net carbs per day) **12** / *Total Daily Net Carbs* **8**

Wednesday

		Net Carbs
Breakfast	Ginger-Basil Avocado Smoothie (page 60)	4
Lunch	Shrimp Tacos with Avocado (page 121)	4
Dinner	Buffalo Chicken Meatloaf Stuffed with Blue Cheese (page 186)	2

Snack Allowance (based on 20 net carbs per day) **10** / *Total Daily Net Carbs* **10**

Thursday

		Net Carbs
Breakfast	Scrambled Cinnamon and Cream Cheese Eggs (page 40)	1
Lunch	Mozzarella Crust Pizza (page 73)	3
Dinner	Cod + Lemon-Ricotta Zoodles (page 97)	4

Snack Allowance (based on 20 net carbs per day) **12** / *Total Daily Net Carbs* **8**

Friday		Net Carbs
Breakfast	Oatless Ricotta Oatmeal (page 32)	1
Lunch	Pulled Buffalo Chicken Salad with Blue Cheese (page 173)	5
Dinner	Garlic and Thyme Skillet Salmon (page 102)	1

Snack Allowance (based on 20 net carbs per day) **13** / *Total Daily Net Carbs* **7**

Saturday		Net Carbs
Breakfast	Lemon-Lavender Ricotta Pancakes (page 33)	2
Lunch	Chili-Lime Drumsticks (page 191)	4
Dinner	Creamy Seafood Chowder (page 112)	4

Snack Allowance (based on 20 net carbs per day) **10** / *Total Daily Net Carbs* **10**

Sunday		Net Carbs
Breakfast	Harvest Omelet (page 41)	3
Lunch	Blue Cheese Beef Roll-Ups (page 140)	1
Dinner	Steak + Perfect Roasted Garlic (page 89)	4

Snack Allowance (based on 20 net carbs per day) **12** / *Total Daily Net Carbs* **8**

Monday

		Net Carbs
Breakfast	Toasted Cinnamon-Vanilla-Coconut Cereal (page 30)	3
Lunch	Blue Cheese Buffalo Chicken Balls (page 188)	2
Dinner	Creamy Langostinos Normandy (page 115)	4

Snack Allowance (based on 20 net carbs per day) **11** / *Total Daily Net Carbs* **9**

Tuesday

		Net Carbs
Breakfast	Oatless Ricotta Oatmeal (page 32)	1
Lunch	Cauliflower Risotto (page 92)	5
Dinner	Chicken + Spicy Buttered Beans (page 90)	4

Snack Allowance (based on 20 net carbs per day) **10** / *Total Daily Net Carbs* **10**

Wednesday

		Net Carbs
Breakfast	Garlic and Thyme Baked Egg (page 35)	1
Lunch	Crisp Bacon and Blue Cheese Zoodles (page 95)	5
Dinner	Pan-Seared Rosemary-Mint Lamb Lollipops (page 147)	2

Snack Allowance (based on 20 net carbs per day) **12** / *Total Daily Net Carbs* **8**

Thursday

		Net Carbs
Breakfast	Salted Chocolate and Macadamia Nut Smoothie (page 62)	1
Lunch	Mini Salami and Cheese Pizzas (page 74)	3
Dinner	Steak + Fresh-Cut Herb and Butter Zoodles (page 98)	6

Snack Allowance (based on 20 net carbs per day) **10** / *Total Daily Net Carbs* **10**

Friday

		Net Carbs
Breakfast	Cinnamon Toast Pork Rinds (page 31)	0
Lunch	Bacon-Ranch Quesadilla with Chicken (page 159)	2
Dinner	Philly Cheesesteak Meatloaf (page 131)	9

Snack Allowance (based on 20 net carbs per day) **9** / *Total Daily Net Carbs* **11**

Saturday

		Net Carbs
Breakfast	Breakfast Tacos (page 45)	1
Lunch	Bacon and Leek Dinner Frittata (page 162)	3
Dinner	Saturday Garlic Shrimp (page 120)	4

Snack Allowance (based on 20 net carbs per day) **12** / *Total Daily Net Carbs* **8**

Sunday

		Net Carbs
Breakfast	Rosemary Quiche (page 44)	1
Lunch	Chicken and Broccoli Alfredo (page 181)	1
Dinner	Chicken Pad Thai (page 93)	8

Snack Allowance (based on 20 net carbs per day) **10** / *Total Daily Net Carbs* **10**

WEEK FOUR

The Dirty Dozen and the Clean Fifteen

A nonprofit and environmental watchdog organization called Environmental Working Group (EWG) looks at data supplied by the US Department of Agriculture (USDA) and the Food and Drug Administration (FDA) about pesticide residues and compiles a list each year of the best and worst pesticide loads found in commercial crops. You can refer to the Dirty Dozen list to know which fruits and vegetables you should always buy organic. The Clean Fifteen list lets you know which produce is considered safe enough when grown conventionally to allow you to skip the organics. This does not mean that the Clean Fifteen produce is pesticide-free, though, so wash these fruits and vegetables thoroughly. These lists change every year, so make sure you look up the most recent before you fill your shopping cart. You'll find the most recent lists as well as a guide to pesticides in produce at www.EWG.org/FoodNews.

2017	
DIRTY DOZEN	**CLEAN FIFTEEN**
Apples	Asparagus
Celery	Avocados
Cherries	Cabbage
Grapes	Cantaloupe
Nectarines	Cauliflower
Peaches	Eggplant
Pears	Grapefruit
Potatoes	Honeydew melon
Spinach	Kiwis
Strawberries	Mangos
Sweet bell peppers	Onions
Tomatoes	Papayas
	Pineapples
In addition to the Dirty Dozen, the EWG added two foods contaminated with highly toxic organo-phosphate insecticides:	Sweet corn
	Sweet peas (frozen)
Hot peppers	
Kale/Collard greens	

APPENDIX C
Conversion Tables

Volume Equivalents (Liquid)

US STANDARD	US STANDARD (OUNCES)	METRIC (APPROXIMATE)
2 tablespoons	1 fl. oz.	30 mL
¼ cup	2 fl. oz.	60 mL
½ cup	4 fl. oz.	120 mL
1 cup	8 fl. oz.	240 mL
1½ cups	12 fl. oz.	355 mL
2 cups or 1 pint	16 fl. oz.	475 mL
4 cups or 1 quart	32 fl. oz.	1 L
1 gallon	128 fl. oz.	4 L

Oven Temperatures

FAHRENHEIT (F)	CELSIUS (C) (APPROXIMATE)
250°	120°
300°	150°
325°	165°
350°	180°
375°	190°
400°	200°
425°	220°
450°	230°

Volume Equivalents (Dry)

US STANDARD	METRIC (APPROXIMATE)
⅛ teaspoon	0.5 mL
¼ teaspoon	1 mL
½ teaspoon	2 mL
¾ teaspoon	4 mL
1 teaspoon	5 mL
1 tablespoon	15 mL
¼ cup	59 mL
⅓ cup	79 mL
½ cup	118 mL
⅔ cup	156 mL
¾ cup	177 mL
1 cup	235 mL
2 cups or 1 pint	475 mL
3 cups	700 mL
4 cups or 1 quart	1 L
½ gallon	2 L
1 gallon	4 L

Weight Equivalents

US STANDARD	METRIC (APPROXIMATE)
½ ounce	15 g
1 ounce	30 g
2 ounces	60 g
4 ounces	115 g
8 ounces	225 g
12 ounces	340 g
16 ounces or 1 pound	455 g

Resources

Books

John Briffa, *Escape the Diet Trap*

William Davis, *Wheat Belly: Lose the Wheat, Lose the Weight, and Find Your Path Back to Health*

Mary Enig and Sally Fallon, *Eat Fat, Lose Fat: The Healthy Alternative to Trans Fats*

Zoë Harcombe, *The Obesity Epidemic*

Lyle McDonald, *The Ketogenic Diet: A Complete Guide for the Dieter and Practitioner*

Jimmy Moore and Eric Westman, *Keto Clarity: Your Definitive Guide to the Benefits of a Low-Carb, High-Fat Diet*

Tim Noakes, Jonno Proudfoot, and Sally-Ann Creed, *The Real Meal Revolution: The Radical Sustainable Approach to Healthy Eating*

David Perlmutter, *Grain Brain: The Surprising Truth about Wheat, Carbs, and Sugar—Your Brain's Silent Killers*

Stephen D. Phinney and Jeff S. Volek, *The Art and Science of Low Carbohydrate Living*

Mark Sisson, *The Primal Blueprint*

Gary Taubes, *Good Calories, Bad Calories: Fats, Carbs, and the Controversial Science of Diet and Health*

Gary Taubes, *Why We Get Fat: And What to Do About It*

Robb Wolf, *The Paleo Solution: The Original Human Diet*

Websites

Ditch the Carbs
ditchthecarbs.com

The Eating Academy by Dr. Peter Attia
eatingacademy.com

Everything about Keto Subreddit
reddit.com/r/keto/

Found My Fitness with Dr. Rhonda Patrick
foundmyfitness.com

I Breathe I'm Hungry
ibreatheimhungry.com

I Quit Sugar
iquitsugar.com

Keto Diet Blog
ketodietapp.com/Blog

Keto Nutrition with Dr. Dominic P. D'Agostino
ketonutrition.org

The Ketogenic Diet for Health
ketotic.org

Ketopia: Wonderful Low-Carb Science
ketopia.com

Livin' La Vida Low-Carb
livinlavidalowcarb.com

Nutrition Science Initiative
nusi.org

The Rosedale Program by Dr. Ron Rosedale
drrosedale.com

Ruling the Keto Diet and Getting in Shape
ruled.me

Up Late Anyway
uplateanyway.com/keto/

References

de Rooy, Laura, and Jane Howdon. "Nutritional Factors That Affect the Postnatal Metabolic Adaptation of Full-Term Small- and Large-for-Gestational-Age Infants." *Journal of Pediatrics* 109, no. 3 (March 2002): pediatrics.aappublications.org/content/109/3/e42.long.

Manninen, Anssi H. "Metabolic Effects of the Very-Low-Carbohydrate Diets: Misunderstood 'Villains' of Human Metabolism." *Journal of the International Society of Sports Nutrition* 1, no. 2 (2004): 7–11. doi:10.1186/1550-2783-1-2-7.

Paoli, A., A. Rubini, J. S. Volek, and K. A. Grimaldi. "Beyond Weight Loss: A Review of the Therapeutic Uses of Very-Low-Carbohydrate (Ketogenic) Diets." *European Journal of Clinical Nutrition* 67, no. 8 (August 2013): 789–96. doi:10.1038/ejcn.2013.116.

Schachter, Steven C., Eric Kossoff, and Joseph Sirven. "Ketogenic Diet." Epilepsy Foundation. August 2013. www.epilepsy.com/learn/treating-seizures-and-epilepsy/dietary-therapies/ketogenic-diet.

Recipe Index

Index

About the Author

 Amanda C. Hughes is a ketogenic chef based in New England with nearly a decade of experience in developing and cooking popular low-carb and paleo recipes. Her ketogenic food adventure blog, **WickedStuffed.com**, has been described as "life-saving," "hilarious," "delicious," and "nonsense free" by the hundreds of thousands of keto-loving home chefs who loyally follow her.